The ANCIENT KEYS of INTERCESSION

A Practical Guide
To Praying Your Church
Into Her Glorious Destiny

AMELDA THOMAS-JONES

The Ancient Keys of Intercession

By

AMELDA THOMAS-JONES

COPYRIGHT © 2018 by
F.A.I.T.H. Clarion Call Publications
P.O. Box 1213
O'Fallon, IL 62269

First Printing, July 2018

ISBN: 978-0-692-14463-3

Unless otherwise identified, Scripture quotations are from THE NEW KING JAMES VERSION of the Bible. Copyright © 1979, 1980, 1982, by Thomas Nelson, Inc., publishers. Used by permission. All rights reserved.

ALL RIGHTS RESERVED

No part of this publication may be reproduced, stored in a retrieval system, or transmitted in any form or by any means—electronic, mechanical, photocopying, recording, or otherwise—without prior written permission from the publisher: F.A.I.T.H. Clarion Call Publications, P.O. Box 1213, O'Fallon, IL 62269. Refer to our website for current information:
www.faithint.org

Printed in the United States of America

Dedication

I dedicate this book to my Lord Jesus Christ, the One who is positioning and preparing His Bride for her glorious destiny.

I also dedicate this book to my grandmother, Cordillia Salomon. She is the one who groomed and cultivated the call to intercession in my life. At age 12, I was given a photograph of me at an early age holding a set of keys.

These keys were given to me by my grandmother as a reminder of the ancient keys of intercession she was imparting to me, according to Jeremiah 6:16.

Thus says the Lord: "Stand in the ways and see, and ask for the old paths, where the good way is, and walk in it; then you will find rest for your souls. . . "

She entrusted these timeless keys of intercession to me because she said, "Those who come behind you, will ask for them. You teach and they will walk in the good way of the ancient path of intercession."

AMELDA THOMAS-JONES

Through the years the photograph has served as a reminder lest I forget the ancient keys entrusted to me. This book is the latest response to my grandmother's call to teach **"The Ancient Keys of Intercession"** to the next generation so they can walk in the ancient and proven paths of intercession.

I consider my grandmother to be the best intercessor I have ever known. She was a hard working woman of integrity with an intimate relationship with the Father, the Son, and the Holy Ghost. I am blessed to have been called by my grandmother a fourth generation intercessor. I loved her with all my heart.

Acknowledgments

First and foremost I thank the Lord for His insight and the Holy Spirit for bringing everything to memory to be able to impart this book into you.

Special thanks to my beloved children Ellis E. Jones, and Leon and Marjorie Hall whose encouragement in recalling the stories prompted me to write this book.

Special thanks to Bishop Geoffrey V. Dudley, Sr., D.Min. (F.A.I.T.H.'s covering); to Dagne Barton, Bishop Dudley's Executive Assistant; to Jason A. Atkinson, Joel and Kellie La Follette, Barbara Evonne Hinson ("Von"), and Kimberly Ellis-Garris, MD, for their contributions; and to Greg and Karen Fry for their tireless support and encouragement in editing this work of the Lord.

Endorsement

Amelda has done it again! She has taken her years of teaching prayer and thousands of miles of traveling all over the world as a literal Pied Piper of prayer and put them in this book. Her insight, revelation, and practical application are summed up in this book. Reading it and applying it will increase your capacity to pray and get answers!

Sincerely Changing Lives for Christ,

Bishop Geoffrey V. Dudley, Sr., D.Min., Senior Pastor
New Life in Christ Interdenominational Church
O'Fallon, Illinois

Foreword

Some people think about praying. Some people talk about praying. Some people say they will pray. Some people pray once in a while. Some people love to pray and actually live a life that progressively becomes a prayer.

Amelda Thomas-Jones is a person who understands the privilege and the power of prayer, and she has been a great blessing and prayer catalyst to me and to our church family. She understands that prayer in its highest form is finding out what God wants to do and then asking Him to do it. People who are Spirit-led in their prayers are discerners, rather than deciders.

This sweet sister communicates and lives prayer. She knows that prayer is warfare and everything else (what we often call ministry) is simply gathering the victor's plunder. True Christ-followers fight from their knees. Amelda teaches people to roll up their sleeves and fall on their knees.

May the words of this book permanently attach themselves to your soul! Hell hopes they won't. Heaven knows they will.

Ken Johnson, former Lead Pastor
Westside Church
Bend, Oregon

Contents

Introduction

The writing of this book is intentional. My main purpose is to leave it as a gift, a legacy for generations to come. These coming generations are not my "tomorrow"—they are my "today." I am compelled of the Lord to train them in hearing and responding to the still small voice of God—a discipline that has spanned the ages and flows out of an intimate relationship with our loving Father God. It is imperative for the intercessor and person of prayer to have this intimate relationship with God because His voice is the only voice we should respond to in preparing the Church for His glorious return.

My mandate from God is to prepare the Church to meet her destiny. Christ will return. He expects the Church to be a certain way: "*...not having spot or wrinkle or any such thing,...*" (Ephesians 5:27)

At age nine, my grandmother mentored and coached me in the ways of intercessory prayer. We never prayed without the Bible open. As God would say something to her, she would go to the Bible and start praying what she was reading. She also taught me how to hear and respond to the voice of God even as Eli did for Samuel.

Now the boy Samuel ministered to the LORD before Eli. And the word of the LORD was rare in those days; there was no widespread revelation ... and while Samuel was lying down, that the LORD called Samuel. And he answered, "Here I am!" So he ran to Eli and said, "Here I am, for you called me." And he said, "I did not call; lie down again." And he went and lay down. Then the LORD called yet again, "Samuel!" So Samuel arose and went to Eli, and said, "Here I am, for you called me." He answered, "I did not call, my son; lie down again." (Now Samuel did not yet know the LORD, nor was the word of the LORD yet revealed to him). And the LORD called Samuel again the third time. So he arose and went to Eli, and said, "Here I am, for you did call me." Then Eli perceived that the LORD had called the boy. Therefore Eli said to Samuel, "Go, lie down; and it shall be, if He calls you, that you must say, 'Speak, LORD, for Your servant hears.'" So Samuel went and lay down in his place. Now the LORD came and stood and called as at other times, "Samuel! Samuel!" And Samuel answered, "Speak, for Your servant hears." Then the LORD said to Samuel: "Behold, I will do something in Israel at which both ears of everyone who hears it will tingle." (1 Samuel 3:1-11)

Rebellious as I may have been, I have never forgotten the tutelage of my grandmother through the years. Today I can still hear the soft voice of my Lord. It is His voice that inspires and directs my prayers—a discipline taught to me by my grandmother. This legacy of hearing and praying the voice of God I have instilled in my biological children and pray that it would now be instilled in you through the reading of this book.

There is no substitute for hearing the voice of God and it is essential in praying the will of God. This gift comes only through knowing Jesus Christ personally as your Savior. So before embarking on this study, I am compelled to ask you, "Do you know Jesus as *your* personal Lord and Savior?"

If you do, we rejoice with you that your name is written in heaven (Luke 10:20). If you do not, we would like to invite you to receive Jesus now, as your Savior. Please join me in praying the following prayer of salvation:

Father, thank You for this opportunity to give my heart to You. Forgive me of my sins. I confess Jesus as Lord and believe that You raised Him from the dead. I believe and receive You in my heart. Now in accordance to Your Word, I thank You I am saved. Amen.

For those who have prayed this prayer from your hearts, we celebrate your spiritual birth into the family of God. Please refer to "Appendix A" for the Scriptural foundation of what has transpired and the assurance you are now reconciled with God the Father and a member of His Church.

Next Step:

Partner with a church who teaches that Jesus is Lord to the glory of God the Father—discipling you to grow in Jesus and Him crucified.

God's Call to the Church:

The Lord is calling the Church to be proactive and disciplined in prayer. This book will focus on four practical areas of how to effectively pray your church into "Her Glorious Destiny:"

1) A Praying Church
2) Praying God's Vision
3) The Place to Pray
4) The Intercessor's Response

God calls us to pray for things both inside and outside the physical walls of the Church. "Appendix B" is an exhortation for those who God is calling to start their own prayer group for things outside or beyond the walls of the Church. This Appendix reveals how these same prayer principles set forth in this study are applicable for: a specific ministry; a school; the military; a friend; government; neighborhood; or whatever prayer burden God has put on your heart.

How to Use This Book:

This is an interactive book which highlights many truths from God's Word. Each shaded box in the text [ ] represents a Scripture you are to research and annotate into the space provided. Each Scriptural reference can then be verified in "Appendix C" at the back of the book.

Take Selah moments. Pause at the end of each chapter and meditate on what you have read. Allow the Holy Spirit to speak and lead you. Slow down and listen for the still small voice of God. Prayerfully consider the study questions and then capture the revelations of the Holy Spirit through journaling. Please refer to "Appendix D" for instructions on how to create your own personal prayer journal so you can learn how to converse and be purposeful to partner with God, not simply hear Him.

This book is meant to be used as a tool as we "*contend earnestly for the faith.*" (Jude 3) My prayer is that this book will equip and encourage you in praying your church into "Her Glorious Destiny."

The following Scripture is the foundational truth to this transforming call to the Church:

"...that He might sanctify and cleanse her
with the washing of water by the word,
that He might present her to Himself
a glorious church, not having spot or wrinkle
or any such thing, but that she should be
holy and without blemish."
Ephesians 5:26-27

Now is the time for generations of praying children, youth, adults, and seniors to rise up and contend together for the glorious destiny of the Church. We serve a God of generations: the God of Abraham, Isaac, and Jacob. To the Builders (the Abrahams) and the Baby Boomers (the Isaacs), the Lord would have me encourage you. We are the generations on whose shoulders the coming generations, our "todays," will stand; we are to be the foundation from which this generation will know their God. "*This is Jacob, the generation of those who seek Him, who seek Your face.*" (Psalms 24:6)

We are to leave them a godly inheritance. It is from this inheritance, and our example, they will become the shoulders to those following them to stand upon to know and serve their God.

Now, may the Church arise in newfound power as the generations prayerfully unite, responding to the voice of God to move into her finest hour, "Her Glorious Destiny"—to become the Bride of Christ!

Prayer of Preparation:

As we now enter into this prayer assignment from God, join me as we ask God to lead us by His Holy Spirit.

Example of Prayers:

Holy Father, we give You thanks. We give You thanks in each area of our lives. Holy Spirit, we ask You to fill us with all truth so we will be able to pray Your will according to Your Word.

Father, we praise You for what You have done. We worship You for Who You are. We believe that as we pray You will open our understanding and that the truth of Your Word will bring illumination so that we will be able to understand Your will as we pray.

Holy Father, open the eyes of our understanding as the Holy Spirit shows Truth to us. Father, we give You thanks. In Jesus' name. Amen!

Matthew 6:9-10 – *"In this manner, therefore, pray: Our Father in heaven, (Let Your name be kept holy, and Let Your name be treated with reverence) Hallowed be Your name. Your kingdom come. Your will be done on earth as it is in heaven."*

Luke 4:1 – *"Then Jesus, being filled with the Holy Spirit, returned from the Jordan and was led by the Spirit into the wilderness,..."*

Ephesians 5:20 – *"...giving thanks always for all things to God the Father in the name of our Lord Jesus Christ;..."*

I would encourage you to pray this or a similar prayer of preparation every time you open this book. This will help you to prepare your heart to hear the voice of God and pray out of the inspiration and direction of His Holy Spirit.

THE FIRST KEY

A Praying Church

"...that He might sanctify and cleanse her with the washing of water by the word, that He might present her to Himself a glorious church, not having spot or wrinkle or any such thing, but that she should be holy and without blemish." **Ephesians 5:26-27**

What is important is knowing in the deepest part of your heart, God hears prayers. He sees. He knows. He cares. Prayer matters. He prepares. He gives tools. God is able to do more than I could have ever imagined. Think about it for a moment. Who gets invited to lead a prayer team when you can't physically attend church or the event you are praying for? How is that even possible? He is God. "Now to Him who is able to do immeasurably more than all we ask or imagine, according to His power that is at work in us, to Him be glory in the church and in Christ Jesus throughout all generations forever and ever! Amen." (Ephesians 3:20-21)

I encourage you to open the pages of this book and know God in ways beyond anything you can currently imagine through prayer. Don't be surprised if your life and the lives of those around you are forever changed as you pray.

Kellie La Follette, Lead Intercessor
West Linn, Oregon

~ 1 ~
God's Divine Call

You are called, I am called. We are all called to pray. Prayer is a weapon, one of the most powerful vehicles the Church has in preparing for the return of Jesus Christ.

The Bible states to *"...pray without ceasing."* 1[ ] Once we, as individuals, accept our role and are fully prepared, it is our individual and corporate responsibility to be a praying church. Then the praying church becomes a powerful living organism armed with the Word of God, and the *"...gates of Hades shall not prevail against it."* 2[ ]

We must stand fast knowing this is not just the role of the intercessor. This is the role of every member of the Church. Special gifts do not preclude you and me from praying. God has called each born again believer to this post of prayer. We cannot relegate it only to a few. We are ALL called. The Scripture makes it clear *"...that men always ought to pray..."* 3[ ] Even though the Scripture calls all of us to pray, *"The heart is deceitful above all things, and desperately wicked; who can know it?"* 4[ ] Hence, the preparation of our heart is important. God needs to prepare our hearts for service to Him. As we allow Him to do that, our prayers will fortify our church and we become a praying church.

Characteristics of a Praying Church:

- A praying church is alive. It knows it is not only operating when prayer is called; it is a way of life and releases transformational change.
- A praying church is a soul winning, living, and breathing organism. It is in *"...Him we live and move and have our being,..."* 5[ ]
- A praying church brings *"...all the tithes..."* 6[ ] into the Church.
- A praying church has *"...each one give as he purposes in his heart..."* 7[ ]

- A praying church gives of their tithes, offerings, and time where they are fed.
- A praying church knows that giving to your church is your responsibility.
- A praying church is an orderly church: timely, loving, helpful, desiring that *"...all things be done decently and in order."* 8[ ]
- A praying church is powerful. *"The effective, fervent prayer of a righteous man avails much."* 9[ ]
- A praying church is intentionally taught. In the daily reading of God's Word, know it goes hand in hand with prayer. These two together cause us to want to be a praying church. *"Be diligent to present yourself approved to God, a worker who does not need to be ashamed, rightly dividing the word of truth."* 10[ ]
- A praying church is in covenant relationship. When we are in covenant with God and one another, the vision to pray for our church becomes natural. It's relational. *"For where two or three are gathered together in My name, I am there in the midst of them."* 11[ ]
- A praying church is *"...to contend earnestly for the faith..."* 12[ ]
- A praying church prays in the name of Jesus. *"And whatever you ask in My name, that I will do..."* 13[ ]
- A praying church fulfills the commandment to *"...love one another...."* 14[ ]
- A praying church contends for the protection of the unborn.
- A praying church cares for one another.
- A praying church does not tolerate injustice.
- A praying church seeks God for His Kingdom to come and His *"...will be done on earth as it is in heaven."* 15[ ]
- A praying church has a strong devotional lifestyle; a lifestyle that rules their lives and permeates into their church, home, marketplace, and beyond.
- A praying church is comprised of individuals with a lifestyle of prayer who do not have to be coerced to enter into prayer.

A church becomes a praying church when the call to pray is obeyed. Then, our prayers begin to flow from the very heart of God—prayers to release the Church into "Her Glorious Destiny."

Selah Moments—pause and meditate: journal personal reflections from the Lord:

____

____

____

____

Study Questions:

1. Can you pause right now and ask God to prepare your heart for the service of prayer. Will you obey?

2. We are <u>all</u> called to pray; are you armed and praying the Word? Share how you are partnering with the Word in prayer.

3. Are you in covenant relationship with God and your church? What does that look like?

4. What would it look like for you to take a step towards *"...praying without ceasing"*? (Thessalonians 5:17)

5. Are you committed to pray on behalf of your church?

Concluding Prayer:

Heavenly Father, I give You thanks I can come to You. I need Your help. Only You can prepare the heart of man. Help me to be in covenant relationship with You as I pray for my church. In Jesus' name. Amen!

~ 2 ~
Why Pray

Prayer is my passion. I've been at this for awhile. Whenever I think of the Lord's return and the condition of the Church, I ask myself the question, "Why isn't the Church praying more?" Don't we realize it is one of the foremost ways we can prepare the Church for His return?

Since 1971, I would find people to pray with. September 7, 1977 while stationed at Howard Air Force Base (AFB) in Panama, I formally started prayer groups wherever we would travel from base to base. It was during the time of the Torrijos-Carter Treaties, formalizing the return of the Panama Canal to the Panamanians. And so, it was done, December 31, 1999, the Panama Canal was officially turned over to Panama. Realizing the Call of God on me after leaving Panama, I realized intercessory prayer is a key to open the arsenal of heaven. Almighty God would select the weapons of our warfare. They are mighty through *"God to the pulling down of strongholds"* (2 Corinthians 10:4). The prerequisite is to be obedient.... After leaving Ramstein AFB in Germany in 1983, I moved to Scott AFB in Illinois. The first thing I did at Scott AFB Chapel was to start a prayer group called, "Father Answers Intercessors Travailing in Holiness" (F.A.I.T.H.). God called F.A.I.T.H. as an Emissary of Intercession to pray for the Armed Forces personnel and their families.

Praying for the Armed Forces personnel and their families by then was innate. The Lord said to me, "I have called F.A.I.T.H. as an Emissary of Intercession for the Department of Defense and their families." It was at that time the Lord illuminated to me, "It was through the Armed Forces 'I' send you along with your family to Europe, the Pacific, the Continental U.S., Alaska, and beyond." Prayer seemed to go wherever I went.

It was at Scott AFB I knew God was calling people of prayer. The group was very strong with people praying Sunday mornings from 6:00 to 7:00.

After we left Scott AFB, F.A.I.T.H. continued and my passion for prayer heightened with subsequent military assignments. To this present day, my passion continues.

Prayer should be purposeful in the Church. The intent is to unite our hearts as we gather. Prayer causes us to focus on the things of God. Prayer opens our heart to the purpose of God and is a guiding force as the Holy Spirit teaches and leads us *"into all truth."* 16[ ]

Reasons to Pray:

The question I am most frequently asked while conducting Prayer Seminars/Workshops is, "Why pray?" I believe the church who prays is a disciplined church. Prayer brings our focus into the place God would have us to be in His affairs. I also believe a church that does not see prayer as a priority is only another social entity. For that matter, any area or ministry of a church that does not open and close with prayer, I believe, does not reverence the Lord.

Prayer in the Church is one of the ways we can ask the Lord to lead and empower us. The Church should be preparing for soul winning revival and discipleship to break out in every area of our churches.

The Following are Foundational Reasons to Pray:

- Why pray? Praying is communicating with God. *"...let your requests be made known to God..."* 17[ ]
- Why pray? Praying the vision God gave the leader of the church (or country, mission, ministry) brings it into existence.
- Why pray? Prayer is seeking and hearing the voice of God for instruction and direction as David did as he *"...inquired of the LORD, saying, 'Shall I pursue this troop? Shall I overtake them?'"* 18[ ]
- Why pray? Prayer is receiving specific instruction from the Lord as we inquire of Him. *"And He answered him, 'Pursue, for you shall surely overtake them and without fail recover all.'"* 19[ ]

- Why pray? Prayer is having the confidence that God will do what He said He will do. *"God is not a man, that He should lie, nor a son of man, that He should repent."* 20[ ]
- Why pray? Prayer is a means of seeking and finding God. *"And you will seek Me and find Me, when you search for Me with all your heart."* 21[ ]
- Why pray? Prayer is a mandate from God. *"I desire therefore that the men pray everywhere, lifting up holy hands, without wrath and doubting;..."* 22[ ]
- Why pray? Prayer is our response to God's desire for us to stand in the gap. *"So I sought for a man among them who would make a wall, and stand in the gap before Me on behalf of the land, that I should not destroy it; but I found no one."* 23[ ]
- Why pray? Prayer leads to godliness and reverence. *"Therefore I exhort first of all that supplications, prayers, intercessions, and giving of thanks be made for all men, for kings and all who are in authority, that we may lead a quiet and peaceable life in all godliness and reverence."* 24[ ]
- Why pray? Prayer is a response to God's call to repentance so He can respond appropriately as we turn from ourselves to Him. Keeping in mind, it is conditional. God said: *"...if My people who are called by My name will humble themselves, and pray and seek My face, and turn from their wicked ways, then I will hear from heaven, and will forgive their sin and heal their land."* 25[ ]

Selah Moments—pause and meditate: journal personal reflections from the Lord:

____

____

____

____

Study Questions:

1. Are you passionate about prayer?

2. Prayer is our response to God's desire for us to stand in the gap. Are you willing to commit to standing in the gap for others?

3. Prayer should be purposeful in the Church. Is your church a place of prayer?

4. What are you focused on today? Will your prayers be a part in preparing hearts for His glorious return?

5. Are you praying for souls? Jesus is returning for a church *"not having spot, or wrinkle, or any such thing; but that it should be holy and without blemish."* (Ephesians 5:27)

6. Part of prayer is listening to the Father. What do you need to do to still yourself and your heart before the Lord in order to hear Him?

Concluding Prayer:

Heavenly Father, give me Your heart to pray according to Your will. Help me to stand in the gap for others to come to Jesus. In Jesus' name. Amen!

~ 3 ~
How to Pray Effectively

DROP THE BAGGAGE! The successful intercessors and people of prayer are those who are navigating through life living without a spirit of offense and following this Scripture:

"Brethren, I do not count myself to have apprehended; but one thing I do, forgetting those things which are behind and reaching forward to those things which are ahead, I press toward the goal for the prize of the upward call of God in Christ Jesus." (Philippians 3:13-14)

This is a must in praying your church into "Her Glorious Destiny." We must be *"...looking unto Jesus, the author and finisher of our faith..."* 26[ ] We must also forgive *"...one another, even as God in Christ forgave you."* 27[ ] It is imperative!

Walk in Purity:

Basic Prayer 101 must be done only one way: with *"...clean hands and a pure heart..."* 28[ ]—bottom line! It is time that we as intercessors and people of prayer stop fooling ourselves. We cannot drink communion having an aught against our brothers and/or sisters fully knowing the schemes and plots we are having in our heart against one another. Get up! Get it right—it is not a bad thing to ask people to forgive you! Do you not know, *"...the Lord looks at the heart."* 29[ ]

Do you not realize, *"Do not be deceived, God is not mocked..."* 30[ ]

Keep a pure heart. Do not harbor hate in your heart for those who have manipulated or said all manner of evil against you. Remember your purpose. People have tried to manipulate me at the altar. I have also had those who lied about me maliciously. In any case, I asked their forgiveness even if I was not in the wrong. We must practice *"...forgiving one another, even as God in Christ forgave you."* 31[ ]

The intercessor and person of prayer must practice Matthew 18 at all times. Their heart motivation must be right toward one another. Never become a stumbling block or ingratiate yourself. The Scripture says, *"If your hand or foot causes you to sin, cut it off and cast it from you."* 32[ ] This does not mean literally cut it off. It is talking about spiritual surgery, mortifying the flesh (your will; your willpower; turning areas over to the Lord and asking Him to help you; your way of thinking as opposed to God's way) and self-denial to obtain eternal life.

Stay Focused:

Keep in mind the winning of souls is very dear to the Lord and thus it should be a priority in our prayers. *"For the Son of Man has come to save that which was lost."* 33[ ]

Seek people to pray with who will help you stand on the Word of God. *"For where two or three are gathered together in My name, I am there in the midst of them."* 34[ ]

Ask God to give you a mentor; not a "yes" person, but one who will mentor you with love and still be able to make the tough calls from the Lord.

Other Considerations:

Always be humble. Be the intercessor and person of prayer who will fall on their faces, humbling themselves before God first. Ask Him for His battle plan, His strategy, and a Word for your situation.

Stay encouraged even when there are not throngs of people in the prayer ministry. Practice connecting with the Lord who *"...always lives to make intercession..."* 35[ ]

Do not exceed your gifting. You cannot take people where you have never been, and/or lead them in areas in which you are unfamiliar. Continue to grow and invest in your gift. Be teachable. Do you know what happens when *"…the blind leads the blind…"* 36[ ] *"Therefore, brethren, be even more diligent to make your call and election sure,…"* 37[ ] Be all that God created you to be in the ministry of prayer.

Selah Moments—pause and meditate: journal personal reflections from the Lord:

____

____

____

____

Study Questions:

1. Have you asked the Lord to give you a heart to forgive as God, for Christ's sake, has forgiven you? Describe how that felt when He forgave you?

2. After reading this chapter, do you see areas where you might have exceeded your gifting? Share an example.

3. Do you have difficulty forgetting those things which are behind? Share an example.

4. *"…the Lord looks at the heart."* (1 Samuel 16:7) Is your heart clean before the Lord? Have you asked Him today to forgive you and purify your heart?

5. Have you sought a mentor who will speak the truth in love to you? If you don't have a mentor, ask God. If you do have a mentor, thank God.

Concluding Prayer:

Heavenly Father, I thank You for giving me a clean heart to navigate out of a spirit of deception. Thank You for a mentor and not a "yes" person. Father, thank You for a heart to pray my church into "Her Glorious Destiny." In Jesus' name. Amen!

~ 4 ~
The Role of the Intercessor

I have often wondered why, of all the gifts the Lord gave the Church, the only one He went to heaven to do is the ministry of intercession. Have you not wondered that also? *"...He always lives to make intercession..."* 38[ ]

The intercessor, while praying their church into "Her Glorious Destiny," should know the vision of their church, keeping in mind the purpose; there is one visionary, the Senior Leader (Senior Pastor or Bishop), or Prayer Lead. And if your church has a Prayer Pastor or Prayer Lead, this is the person to keep God's vision alive for new people to pray into.

What is an Intercessor?

I heard the word intercession before I could spell the word. There are some who say to me, "I'm not an intercessor" or "How do I know I'm an intercessor?" My response is always the same: "Pray, ask the Holy Spirit to lead you. He will; you will not have to conjure up anything." In Ezekiel it says, the Lord *"...sought for a man among them who would...stand in the gap...; but I found no one."* 39[ ] If He sought for someone to pray and make up the hedge, then He will provide for you how to pray.

Know that intercessory prayer is the unseen support structure. Each time I look at the support beams and metal rods of a new building going up, I'll say to myself, "That's the intercessor or person of prayer; the area no one sees." It is the inner structure of a new building that must pass rigorous inspections to see if it will stand the test of time. And it is the same for intercessors. The intercessor must be flexible like the earthquake-proofed buildings—bend under pressure, but do not break!

There are many people standing on the shoulders of intercessors and people of prayer. The weight of the call sometimes will make the intercessor want to break; but they are connected with the Chief Intercessor, Jesus Christ, Who will pray them through.

Having said that, realize this is vital. Trust me. You do not have to be seen or heard by man to be effective. When it is all said and done, it is the motivation of your heart that will be in question. If God wants you to be known, you will be. *"A man's gift makes room for him, and brings him before great men."* 40[ ]

Character of an Intercessor:

Intercessors, people of prayer, and the whole Body of Christ should continually be pursuing the Lord Jesus Christ with *"...clean hands and a pure heart..."* 41[ ] before God. Don't seek the approval of man.

Let's settle a long-standing dispute that I have heard in churches for some time. People would make this statement to me, "I am not an intercessor" or "I am an intercessor." The one who says, "I am not an intercessor" at times may feel insignificant or inferior. That person may even be afraid; intimidated to pray where others may hear them. There may be occasions when others lord over the one who already is feeling unqualified to pray. This is wrong. Being an intercessor does not give us a license above others. Instead, we should always encourage and edify those we pray with.

Could it be that while looking for the intercessors to make up the hedge, God could not find one because they were having arguments—comparing themselves and lording over the people of God? Do not compare yourselves. Greatness is not how you lord over the people of God. Greatness comes out of a servants' heart. Your effectiveness in praying your church into "Her Glorious Destiny" comes from a spirit of humility. *"...he who is greatest among you, let him be as the younger, and he who governs as he who serves."* 42[ ]

We intercessors need not to fight amongst ourselves. If you have a dispute against your brother, settle it among yourselves. *"If he hears you, you have gained your brother."* 43[ ] *"But if he will not hear, take with you one or two more, that 'by the mouth of two or three witnesses every word may be established.'"* 44[ ] Keep no animosity or spirit of offense in your heart against each other; *"...forgiving one another, even as God in Christ also forgave you."* 45[ ]

In the spiritual kingdom, humility and service enjoin a servant's heart. Intercessors and people of prayer should be quick to repent and ask for forgiveness, *"...endeavoring to keep the unity of the Spirit in the bond of peace."* 46[ ]

Everyone is called to pray our churches into her glorious destiny, *"...that He might sanctify and cleanse her with the washing of water by the word, that He might present her to Himself a glorious church, not having spot or wrinkle or any such thing, but that she should be holy and without blemish."* 47[ ] This Scripture is not just for us to pray for the Church; but it has personal application for us, the intercessor, and people of prayer.

Come before God clean. *"Be holy, for I am holy."* 48[ ] There should be no power struggle in the Body of Christ. We have a world to be praying for to come to the knowledge of God. Keep in mind that *"...we do not wrestle against flesh and blood..."* 49[ ] People of God should come clean. *"If we confess our sins..."* 50[ ]

Take the Word of God: *"Put on the whole armor of God..."* 51[ ] while we *"...contend earnestly for the faith..."* 52[ ] Also, *"...do not worry about how or what you should speak."* 53[ ] The Lord will equip you to pray.

Your confidence is in Jesus Christ. He will build your character. Be a team player. Never allow your mouth to cause you to sin. While others are praying, you come in the power of agreement in the name of Jesus. You do not have to have the last word in prayer or pray everything.

Practical Guidelines for an Intercessor:

The following are guidelines for fulfilling the role of an intercessor:

- Do not seek or want one-on-one time with the pastor or key leaders for personal favor.
- Do not seek recognition.
- Do not be offended if not recognized.
- Do not ingratiate yourself with others in order to gain attention, position, status, favor, or power.
- Speak the truth in love at all times.
- *"Be kindly affectionate to one another..."* 54[ ]
- Do not be envious or jealous of another person's position.
- Do not compromise yourself with God or lie to gain favor. What you have done in secret, your heavenly Father knows how to reward you openly, if He chooses. *"...pray to your Father...; and your Father who sees in secret will reward you openly."* 55[ ]
- Do not be prideful about sharing the victories God used you to pray in.
- Be strong, *"You shall not be afraid of the terror by night, nor of the arrow that flies by day,..."* 56[ ]
- Pray for the Godhead to guide you.

Having said all of this, let us take hold of the promises of God with full assurance knowing we are co-laboring in intercession with the Lord, Who forever lives to make intercession for us. Together we are preparing His Church for His return which is "Her Glorious Destiny!"

Selah Moments—pause and meditate: journal personal reflections from the Lord:

____

____

____

____

Study Questions:

1. Do you know the vision for your church? What is it?

2. Describe the role of an intercessor.

3. Ezekiel 22:30 says, the Lord *"sought for a man among them who would... stand in the gap...; but found no one."* If the Lord was searching now, would He find you standing in the gap on behalf of His church and His children? Describe what that intercession looks like in your life.

4. Respond to the statement: "You do not have to be seen or heard by man to be effective."

5. What does it mean to you to pray and not to be looking for the approval of man?

6. How do you continually pursue *"clean hands and a pure heart?"* (Psalms 24:4)

7. From the **"Practical Guidelines for an Intercessor"** section, identify which guideline(s) are areas that you personally need to be particularly aware of. Why?

8. What does it look like in your life to co-labor in intercession with the Lord?

Concluding Prayer:

Heavenly Father, thank You for having provided this practical guide to instruct me in the ways of intercession and prayer. I acknowledge these areas (list them by name) in which I need Your Spirit to teach and guide me. Fill me with Your Spirit so that I may co-labor with You. In Jesus' name. Amen!

THE SECOND KEY

Praying God's Vision

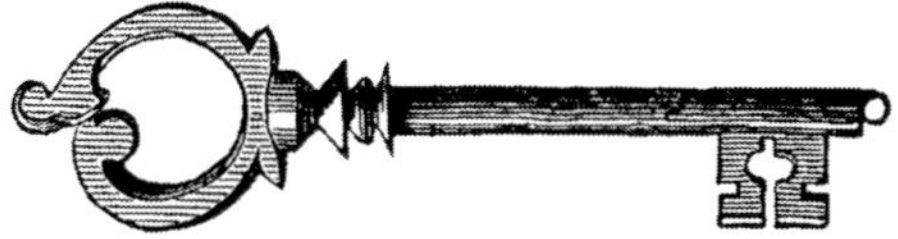

Then the LORD answered me and said: "Write the vision and make it plain on tablets, that he may run who reads it. For the vision is yet for an appointed time; But at the end it will speak, and it will not lie. Though it tarries, wait for it; Because it will surely come, it will not tarry. "Behold the proud, his soul is not upright in him; But the just shall live by his faith." **Habakkuk 2:2-4**

The Ancient Keys of Intercession is more than a book. It is a practical guide to train the Church how to pray in accordance with the Father's will. Filled with Scripture, Amelda Thomas-Jones is setting forth a practical foundation of prayer – praying the Word of God back to the Father.

As a prayer pastor, this book has condensed over a decade of prayer ministry into four essential elements to position the Church to come into Her glorious destiny. It has been an invaluable tool for my own personal growth as an intercessor as well as to serve the vision of the local church, while equipping the next generation of intercessors.

This is not just a good read, but a must read for those responding to God's invitation to participate in what He is doing now.

Greg Fry, Prayer Pastor
Bend, Oregon

~ 5 ~
God's Vision for Your Church

Every church has its own individual fingerprint, or DNA, from the Lord. It is what makes that church unique; just like no two snowflakes are alike, there are no two churches alike. They may look similar; however, there is that "something" that they are known for that makes them unique, a one of a kind. It is what God has created them to be so they can accomplish what God has called them to do. Do you know the uniqueness and God's vision for your church?

If so, every one of us should be able to pray. God has called us, His Body, to always pray. Therefore, wanting to pray for a glorious Church should be our delight knowing He is returning for a Church *"...not having spot, or wrinkle, or any such thing; but that she should be holy and without blemish."* 57[ ]

When you know God's vision for your church you can pray more effectively and informed. Therefore, every one of us should be able to pray in that manner.

"I will stand my watch and set myself on the rampart, and watch to see what He will say to me, and what I will answer when I am corrected. Then the LORD answered me and said: 'Write the vision and make it plain on tablets, that he may run who reads it. For the vision is yet for an appointed time; but at the end it will speak, and it will not lie. Though it tarries, wait for it; because it will surely come, it will not tarry.'" (Habakkuk 2:1-3)

"I will stand my watch and set myself on the rampart,..."
I believe the Sovereign One is saying this to me as I stand my watch. This is the season the Lord God Almighty is calling me to give confidence and support; to persuade, advance, promote His intercessors and people of prayer to pray His vision He has entrusted to His leader(s).

"...and watch to see what He will say to me,..."
For years I was invited to do a TV interview. I did not feel qualified or competent with godly character to do so. Praise the Lord, but they waited; and when the Lord released me after all these years, I did the interview. Not knowing He, the Omniscient God, had a plan and purpose for it.

"...and what I will answer when I am corrected."
If you will Google "AMELDA THOMAS-JONES the Dove," you will see the interview. The Lord spoke through the prophet:

- *"Then the LORD answered me and said:*
- *'Write the vision and make it plain on tablets,*
- *That he may run who reads it.'"*

After we heard the vision of God, we asked our Heavenly Father to show us how to pray and He did. We then prayed what the Lord had given. First and foremost, we started with thanksgiving for His vision. He entrusted it to someone who for years just needed intercessors to come alongside and pray it through. That was us.

We did not expand, interpret, or revise the vision. We just prayed it through as it was given. Hence, we interceded giving thanks to the Lord who gave the vision to His chosen leader, the visionary He entrusted it to.

Selah Moments—pause and meditate: journal personal reflections from the Lord:

____

____

____

____

Study Questions:

1. Do you know the vision God gave your church? Can you share it?

2. How are you partnering with God for the vision?

3. If you are a media church member (i.e., streaming via the internet, Church TV…), do you know the vision God gave them? Share how God would have you to pray.

4. Have you been giving thanksgiving to God for His vision? Pray a prayer of thanksgiving now.

Concluding Prayer:

Heavenly Father, like Habakkuk, show me how to partner with You in prayer for Your vision You have entrusted to my leader; until it becomes a reality. In Jesus' name. Amen!

Be encouraged!

I waited from September 7, 1977 until December 31, 1999 for the Panama Canal Treaty. But the vision of God will surely come to pass.

Then the LORD answered me and said: "Write the vision and make it plain on tablets, that he may run who reads it. For the vision is yet for an appointed time; but at the end it will speak, and it will not lie. ***Though it tarries, wait for it;*** *because it will surely come, it will not tarry."* (Habakkuk 2:2-3)

~ 6 ~
God's Visionary

To every leader God has called, He will give a vision. There is a reason why the Omniscient, all-knowing God would do that. He has entrusted His leader with His vision to do His work here on earth. Every leader called of God is a visionary who is anointed to receive and then fulfill God's vision.

Identify your Visionary:

The visionary of your church is the Senior Leader, the Senior Pastor or Bishop, that has been given the vision from God for the church. THE VISION SHOULD BE WRITTEN PLAINLY. The visionary could be you, the prayer group lead God has called and purposefully gave His vision. We must realize prayer does not take place only within the confines of the church and homes... but in the marketplace, in schools and so on…

First, be assured that God has placed you under the visionary you have and in the church you are in. THE VISION SHOULD BE WRITTEN AND ABLE TO BE ARTICULATED BY EVERY NEW PERSON IN THE GROUP! When you know you are under God's choice of visionary, you can pray with due diligence and very effectively for him/her. This same principle applies to your prayer group or if you are the visionary God has called.

In the case of some churches, spouses are sharing the call of visionary as co-pastors. You will then pray for them both with thoroughness and attentiveness in the Spirit of the loving God! Do not pray carelessly for your visionary!

Pray with Fervor:

Pray with conviction for your visionary—with total abandonment, for he/she is the one who is carrying the vision for the church! *"The effective, fervent prayer of a righteous man avails much. Elijah was a man with a nature like ours, and he prayed earnestly that it would not rain; and it did not rain on the land for three years and six months. And he prayed again, and the heaven gave rain, and the earth produced its fruit."* 58[ ] We call forth that level of intercessor and person of prayer who will pray with fervor for their visionary. Pray like Elijah for your visionary. He is the one God has given the mandate to prepare the church that God has given him. This kind of fervent prayer will prepare your church for "Her Glorious Destiny."

Praying this way is easy if you know this is God's church for you. *"And I will give you shepherds according to My heart,..."* 59[ ]

Pray with Purity:

Pray with clean hands and a pure heart for your visionary and you will be brought into covenant relationship with God and your visionary. A covenant relationship must not be tarnished with an ingratiated spirit. This will be discussed more fully in Chapter 12—Covenant Relationship.

Pray for your visionary! Never forget—there is only one visionary: the Bishop or Senior Pastor. Be careful. Do not try to manipulate your visionary in prayer. When you don't know what to pray, simply pray *"Your kingdom come, Your will be done on earth as it is in heaven"* 60[ ] for your visionary and your church!

Know the Body of believers the Lord has placed you in. This will cause you to pray more effectively for your church and your visionary who is leading the church. Praying for your visionary has nothing to do with whether you like him/her or not. You are mandated by God to pray for *"...all who are in authority,..."* 61[ ]

I have seen people manipulate others through prayer and run to the visionary whispering untruth. Please don't you be guilty of that sin. Do not assassinate the visionary with your tongue. The tongue has two powers: *"Death and life are in the power of the tongue,..."* 62[ ]

Pray with Humility:

I have also seen the visionary so downtrodden because of so-called know-it-all intercessors. It's like none other. I've seen and ministered to visionaries hurt by these so-called intercessors and people of prayer in the churches. Tongues should be guarded, and we should speak with a spirit of love in every instance.

The intercessors are not the only ones who hear from the Lord. Allow the visionary the respect to know they hear from the Lord, too. When something is said or "a word" is delivered to him/her, it should be confirming or give them time to put it on the shelf and process whatever information they received.

Intercessors and people of prayer are not the final authority of the church. We must have respect for the spiritual authority that God has placed over us.

Pray with Purpose:

Pray the Word over and for your visionary. Lift him/her up to always hear a Word from the Lord to feed and lead God's people. Pray that your visionary's ear is always close to the mouth of God.

Pray the Aarons and Hurs will come forth to hold up his/her hands. Pray for the spirit of helps, just as Jethro called forth for Moses, to come and assist your visionary for what God has called him/her to do!

Pray for the spirit of a Jonathan to be sent to come alongside your visionary to minister to him/her as he did for David. Pray insight to be given to the armor bearers to operate as Jonathans! In praying for your visionary, you must also include the paid staff and volunteers. They are a type of Jonathan to your visionary.

Pray Blessings:

Pray and speak blessings into your visionary's life; that *"...blessings shall come upon you and overtake you,..."* 63[ ]

When you start praying blessings for your visionary, things start happening for you that you cannot explain. In praying for my visionary, I have seen the windows of heaven open on my behalf and God has poured out on me *"...such blessing that there will not be room enough to receive it."* 64[ ]

Praying blessings for your visionary gives you peace of mind because you are walking in integrity before God. Pray blessings for him/her. *"The blessings of the Lord makes one rich, and He adds no sorrow with it."* 65[ ]

It is a powerful thing to pray Scriptures and release God's promises over your visionary, especially when you can personalize these prayers by inserting their name into the Scripture. Insert your visionary's name into these Scriptures:

- Prayers for Revelation:
  Ephesians 1:15-23; Colossians 1:9-14; Ephesians 3:14-19
- Prayers for Blessings:
  3 John 2-4; Deuteronomy 28:2; Numbers 6:24-26
- Prayers for Favor:
  Proverbs 13:15; Proverbs 14:35; Luke 2:52

Specific Prayers:

- Pray for your visionary that God's *"...will be done on earth..."* 66[ ] in his/her life as it has already been ordained in heaven by Almighty God.
- Pray for your visionary to walk in accordance with 3 John 2, to *"prosper in all things and be in health, even as (their) soul prospers."*

- Pray for your visionary that *"...the peace of God, which surpasses all understanding, will guard..."* 67[ ] his/her heart and mind through Christ Jesus.
- Pray for your visionary to always have the time for hearing a fresh Word from the Lord to feed you: *"And I will give you shepherds according to My heart, who will feed you with knowledge and understanding."* 68[ ]
- Pray for your visionary to be a weapon in God's hand, therefore: *"No weapon formed against you shall prosper,..."* 69[ ]
- Pray for your visionary to live in joy: *"...In Your presence is fullness of joy; at Your right hand are pleasures forevermore."* 70[ ]
- Pray for your visionary to always have intimate time with the Lord in worship: *"...for the Father is seeking such..."* 71[ ]
- Pray for your visionary and his/her family. Pray for your first lady. In the event she is a co-pastor, pray for her anyway. She is a wife also. Pray that the Lord blesses and heals them! Pray for blessings, success, and victory in their child or children's lives!

Your visionary is a gift and the one entrusted with receiving and fulfilling God's vision for your church. One of the greatest prayers for your visionary is that the church would follow him/her: follow in pursuing God's vision and follow in moving closer to "Her Glorious Destiny." Paul wrote to Timothy to commit the vision *"...to faithful men who will be able to teach others also."* 72[ ] The apostles instructed the early Church to *"...seek out from among you seven men of good reputation, full of the Holy Spirit and wisdom, whom we may appoint over this business; but we will give ourselves continually to prayer and to the ministry of the word."* 73[ ]

The visionary is called to be in God's presence and receive revelation for the church. However, if the church doesn't respond and do their part, the visionary cannot do his/her part. Pray for the church to respond and the visionary to receive.

Selah Moments—pause and meditate: journal personal reflections from the Lord:

____

____

____

____

Study Questions:

1. Can you identify your visionary?

2. Share ways you are partnering with God on behalf of your visionary.

3. Are you praying for the spirit of a covenant relationship, like a Jonathan, to come alongside your visionary?

4. Have you prayed for your visionary and his/her family lately?

5. Have you prayed that your visionary would walk in wisdom and 3 John 2?

6. Has God prompted your visionary to know you are praying for what God has called him/her to do? Will your visionary say something about you like this? ***"... your gift of prayer is what has covered me and my ministry."*** Thank you, Bishop Geoffrey V. Dudley, Sr., D.Min.

Concluding Prayer:

Heavenly Father, forgive me for the times I have neglected to pray for my visionary. Give me a heart of conviction to pray for my visionary and with fervor for the vision You have given until it becomes a reality. In Jesus' name. Amen!

~ 7 ~
The Prayer Pastor/Leader

I realize the concept of a Prayer Pastor is new to some. Yet, I believe it is greatly needed today to pray your church into "Her Glorious Destiny." The Prayer Pastor is one of the two pillars to hold up the arms of the visionary—similar to Aaron and Hur holding up the arms of Moses. Moses was able to execute the things of God for the children of Israel in battle because of the assistance of Aaron and Hur. Our visionary can experience similar victories for his/her church today, with the help of a Prayer Pastor (Aaron) and an Executive Pastor (Hur).

Qualities of a Prayer Pastor:

Over the past thirty-nine years of ministering in a variety of churches around the world, I have realized there is a great need within some churches for a Prayer Pastor. This is a position for an experienced person who has a personal covenant relationship with God and with the visionary of the church.

Qualifications should include a Kingdom mindset and a deep knowledge of spiritual authority. This person is one who would *"...seek first the kingdom of God and His righteousness,..."* 74[ ] and not the internet. Also, they should practice a life of prayer and fasting.

The Prayer Pastor should have the heart of the visionary, as well as a heart to cover the leadership of the church. Keep in mind that this is all done behind the scenes like the unseen inner structure of a building.

Praying for the Vision:

The visionary cannot do it all. Help is needed to lead the church and to keep the vision before the people. *"...write the vision and make it plain on tablets, that he may run who reads it."* 75[ ] This is where the

Prayer Pastor comes in *"For the vision is yet for an appointed time; but at the end it will speak, and it will not lie."* 76[ ] The Prayer Pastor oversees praying the vision into fruition.

What is the unique fingerprint of your church to fulfill God's vision? Who is "making it plain?" Who is being equipped to "run that reads it?" Are we preparing a generation to "make it plain" and "run with it?" There should be no confusion in the Prayer Pastors' mind of the church's vision they are called to because he/she is the one to make it plain to the intercessors and keep them focused and united.

The Prayer Pastor stewards the vision for the church through prayer, coordinating prayer assignments among the ministries of the church and the congregation.

Praying for the Visionary:

The visionary should be free to prepare the Word of God and feed the people of God. The Prayer Pastor assists in leading the church and has his/her eyes on the things of the Spirit concerning the visionary. He/she oversees the prayer covering for the visionary and for the church.

The visionary needs help. In most cases they are apprehensive to ask. Prayer covering is absolutely necessary for the one receiving the vision from God and in spiritual authority; and the Prayer Pastor is the one who coordinates that effort. This is not a position of friendship or ingratiating with the visionary—it is one of servanthood.

Raising up Prayer Leaders:

A primary function of the Prayer Pastor is to raise up prayer leaders for each ministry of the church so they have their own prayer coverage. I believe all ministries of the church should have someone to lead that area in prayer. These individuals should be equipped by the Prayer Pastor to raise up intercessors and people of prayer in their own areas of ministry. The prayer activities of these ministry prayer leaders would be coordinated and supported by the Prayer Pastor.

The Role of Aaron and Hur:

The Executive Pastor leads the church in administrative and logistical functions making sure everyone is in place and the church is running at its optimum capability.

These two positions of the Prayer Pastor and the Executive Pastor represent the Aaron and Hur for the visionary. They will also keep each other from being overly tasked. These are not sought out positions. These are positions directed by the Lord to the visionary.

Aaron and Hur each had the ear of Moses. The Prayer Pastor stands close to the visionary, being sensitive to the things of the Spirit, ministering in the *"...Spirit of wisdom and understanding, the Spirit of counsel and might,..."* 77[ ] This position is accomplished before the Lord God Almighty by fasting, intercession, and travailing on behalf of the visionary.

I realize not all churches will have these positions of a Prayer Pastor and an Executive Pastor. In the event the church does, there should be no competition between these two key positions. They both protect and cover the visionary while being led by the Holy Spirit. They offer suggestions to the visionary in line with the unique fingerprint and God's vision for their individual church.

They both know there is only one visionary directed by God. They will not seek alliance with other members of the congregation or outside the church against the visionary. Total loyalty to the visionary and God's vision for the church is a must!!!

Praying your church into "Her Glorious Destiny" is accomplished by keeping *"...the unity of the Spirit in the bond of peace."* 78[ ] Yes, *"...the kingdom of heaven suffers violence, and the violent take it by force."* 79[ ] This is toward the enemy of the Church, Satan, and not each other. Just like the visionary cannot be everywhere, neither can the Prayer Pastor or the Executive Pastor. Your help is needed to advance the Kingdom of God.

I thank God for Prayer Pastors who are called day and night like a type of Nehemiah, building and protecting *"...so that with one hand they worked at construction, and with the other held a weapon."* 80[ ] The enemy comes with that spirit of discouragement to bring him/her down from constructing the wall of the vision. But they will stand fast even when tested, staying on the wall to prayerfully watch over the vision. With the Prayer Pastor being a strong steward of the vision, he/she is helping the visionary get the job done; fulfilling God's vision and releasing the church into "Her Glorious Destiny."

Selah Moments—pause and meditate: journal personal reflections from the Lord:

____

____

____

____

Study Questions:

1. How has the Prayer Pastor articulated the vision God gave your visionary for your church?

2. How is the Prayer Pastor executing the vision for your church?

3. As Aaron and Hur literally held up the hands of Moses, name three ways your Prayer Pastor is showing you how to hold up your visionary's hands.

4. Moses could execute things of God because of the assistance of Aaron and Hur. Name some of the ways you are supporting your Prayer Pastor to pray for the vision God gave your visionary.

5. Are all ministries in your church covered by prayer?

6. Your help is needed to advance the Kingdom of God to be all it can be. Are you willing to stand fast on the wall watching over the vision?

7. What would it look like for you to take that step?

Concluding Prayer:

Heavenly Father, holy is Your Name. Thank You for a great team of intercessors and people of prayer to advance Your vision in our church. We continually pray for wisdom for our visionary in executing Your vision. In Jesus' name. Amen!

THE THIRD KEY

The Place to Pray

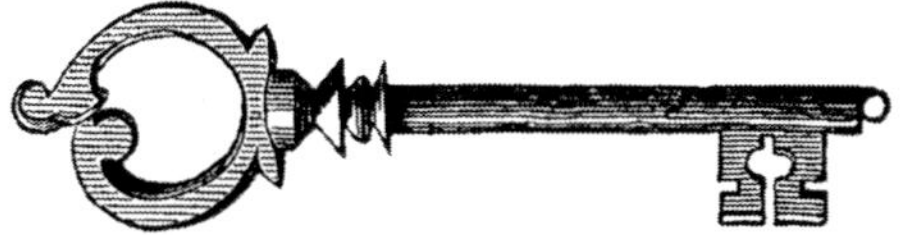

"Pray without ceasing." **1 Thessalonians 5:17**

This book has become my manual for effective ministry. After reading this book from cover to cover – twice, underlining and highlighting passages, dissecting chapters and focusing on specific sections – I am fully persuaded it is the voice of the Holy Spirit through Amelda Thomas-Jones to the Body of Christ.

I apply and implement the Biblical principles from this text not only to my personal ministry, but to my local, jurisdictional, and national ministry assignments as well. This book goes beyond a nice Christian read, because it is an instrument that provides practical and fundamental, step-by-step instructions to edify the Church.

Joanna Coles, Lead Intercessor
Lorton, Virginia

~ 8 ~
Purpose of the Place to Pray

The purpose of the place to pray is to provide a location and atmosphere where we can consistently pray God's will. Pray in accordance with Scripture(s) and don't give up! Consistent prayer is key! *"Then Jesus told His disciples a parable to show them that they should always pray and not give up."* (Luke 18:1)

The place to pray is anywhere and anytime the Spirit of the Lord calls us to pray. This can be in a church, in someone's home, in the marketplace, in a government building, or in a school.

There are four key considerations regarding selecting a place to pray: find a consistent location; determine when to pray; communicate expectations; and establish decorum. The remaining portion of this chapter is devoted to discussing these four key considerations in the context of a church prayer room and praying for the worship service. Even though we are talking specifically about a church prayer room, these considerations are applicable to every place we gather to pray.

1) Find a consistent location:

Intercessors and people of prayer should know the Prayer Room's exact location beforehand. It should not be changed at the last minute without their prior knowledge.

2) Determine when to pray:

The time is during the services. For each worship service, there should be at least two people of the same gender scheduled. For any other prayer assignments using the Prayer Room, secure the time and be consistent, know the purpose, remain focused, and pray in the name of Jesus.

3) Communicate expectations:

Have clearly defined expectations that are understood. Those praying must have a willingness to pray and not gossip. They should be in the Prayer Room at least fifteen minutes prior to prayer time clothed in integrity and equipped with their Bible, bottled drinking water, and breath mints.

4) Establish decorum:

The Prayer Room has a decorum of good manners, good behavior, modesty, respectability, correctness, demureness, etiquette, and restraints which will not be abandoned! The decorum of the intercessor or person of prayer in the Prayer Room should be one devoted to the reading of the Word, one who has an intimate relationship with the Godhead, and one who is in love with the Lord since *"We love Him because He first loved us."* 81[ ]

Types of Prayer:

There are specific types of prayer that should be covered from the Prayer Room during every worship service. These include, but are not limited to, the following:

- **Praise the Lord:** Start with adorations, praise, and thanksgiving.
- **Pray for direction:** Ask the Lord to speak, giving you direction to pray.
- **Pray against hindrances:** Ask the Lord to remove all hindrances that would keep anyone from receiving and responding to the preached/ taught Word of God in the house! God promises that His Word *"...shall not return to Me void..."* 82[ ]
- **Pray for fruit:** That everyone involved in the worship service would be *"...fruitful in every good work and increasing in the knowledge of God;..."* 83[ ]
- **Pray for salvation:** People, *"...do not harden your hearts..."* 84[ ] and respond to the Word.
- **Pray for deliverance:** That people would have their hearts open to the truth, *"...and the truth shall make you free."* 85[ ]

- **Pray for healing:** That people would come, be healed and set free. *"Therefore if the Son makes you free, you shall be free indeed."* 86[ ]
- **Pray for peace:** That people would find peace, *"...that He might reconcile them both to God..."* 87[ ]
- **Pray for God's will:** Petition God for the individual needs of the people including jobs, home, and family. *"Your Kingdom come. Your will be done on earth as it is in heaven."* 88[ ]
- **Pray for signs and wonders:** *"And these signs will follow those who believe: In My name they will..."* 89[ ]
- **Pray with confidence:** *"Now this is the confidence that we have in Him, that if we ask anything according to His will, He hears us. And if we know that He hears us, whatever we ask, we know that we have the petitions that we have asked of Him."* 90[ ]

What a blessing to partner with God, our Heavenly Father, in the ministry of prayer. This we can do with full assurance knowing God will use our prayer time in the Prayer Room to release our church into "Her Glorious Destiny!"

Selah Moments—pause and meditate: journal personal reflections from the Lord:

____

____

____

____

Study Questions:

1. Pause and picture a church that is covered in prayer from the parking lot to the benediction. Whether or not your church has a Prayer Room at this time, will you pray for God's purposes to come forth and pierce the hearts of men, women, and children in the service?

2. Considerations for a Prayer Room include: consistent location, a set time, clear expectations, and an established decorum. If your church has a Prayer Room, are all of these considerations in place?

3. Prayerfully consider if any adjustments are needed.

4. If your church doesn't yet have a Prayer Room, will you seek the Lord for discernment and direction? Explain the direction the Lord gave you.

5. We have read about the specific types of prayers and Scriptures for the Prayer Room, including starting with praising the Lord. Write a prayer of adoration, praise and thanksgiving to the Lord. Search for a Scripture that you can include with your prayer of praise.

Concluding Prayer:

Father in heaven, holy is Your Name. Thank You for the opportunity to pray Your heart through Your Word, for souls to be won, lives delivered, and bondages broken. *"Bless the LORD, O my soul: and all that is within me, bless His holy name."* (Psalms 103:1) We give You praise, O Lord, Your purpose is being fulfilled. In Jesus' name. Amen!

~ 9 ~
Who Should be in the Church Prayer Room

Each person in the Prayer Room should be there to pray for God's purposes to be fulfilled through the worship service.

The Prayer Pastor (or member of the clergy, if the church doesn't have a Prayer Pastor), or their designee, is the first line of defense for authorizing who is to pray in the Prayer Room.

Intercession During the Worship Service:

Everyone with a desire to pray for your church should have access to the Prayer Room once they are trained on the protocol and expectations of praying in the Prayer Room.

There should be regularly scheduled prayer teams for each service made up of a minimum of two to three individuals of the same gender.

Also, every church ministry should have someone praying in the Prayer Room to specifically cover that ministry.

Ministry After the Worship Service:

Only trained ministers should pray for people when brought to the Prayer Room after responding to the preached Word. Everyone else should continue in prayer as the ministry takes place.

Other Times of Prayer:

Praying in the Prayer Room is not an affirmation you are called to the Clergy. We are all called to pray. Each prayer assignment for the Prayer

Room should be scheduled through the clergy-designated person and each person praying should be notified in advance.

Preparing to Pray:

Whenever you go to the Prayer Room, your sins should have been taken care of prior to leaving your home; or, at least, get it done while on your way to church. *"Search me, O God, and know my heart;..."* 91[ ]

Come prepared with *"...clean hands and a pure heart,..."* 92[ ] so you can hear from God and pray His heart for the service.

Don't be late. Being late is not fashionable—it is disrespectful! Not showing up without making arrangements for a replacement shows lack of integrity; not to man, but to God!!

If you should find yourself the only one in the Prayer Room praying, know that you are not alone. You have the Chief Intercessor in agreement with you on behalf of the service! This is not a license for you not to show up and partner on your designated Sunday. Rather, it is to serve as an encouragement that the Lord *"...will never leave you nor forsake you."* 93[ ] However, there are circumstances beyond our control that can cause us not to be in the Prayer Room. Always alert the Prayer Pastor, or his/her designee, if you are not able to fulfill your assignment.

Now is the Time to Pray:

It is a blessing to be standing in prayer for whatever service we are called to pray for. Just imagine the power of connecting with other believers in prayer. Can you sense the connection between you and the One who forever lives to make intercession for the saints?

You are trained. Your heart is prepared. Your love for the work of God is proof He has equipped you. Come with confidence into the Prayer Room to pray your church into "Her Glorious Destiny."

Selah Moments—pause and meditate: journal personal reflections from the Lord:

____

____

____

____

Study Questions:

1. If your church has a Prayer Room, name the delegated authority who would assign you to the Prayer Room.

2. Write a brief description of the position that could be used to invite people to pray in the Prayer Room and from what position(s) in the church.

3. Everyone is called to pray. Beyond that, are you being called to serve in the Prayer Room?

4. Are all ministries in your church covered with someone praying specifically for each ministry? Are there any gaps that need prayer coverage?

5. What would it take to identify and fill the gaps so that every ministry is covered in prayer?

6. What do you need to do, prior to arriving at the Prayer Room, to have *"...clean hands and a pure heart,..."*? (Psalms 24:4)

7. If you are ever physically alone in the Prayer Room, you are never alone when you pray. The Chief Intercessor is with you. How does knowing Hebrews 13:5 *"...I will never leave you or forsake you"* affect your heart to pray for the service?

Concluding Prayer:

Heavenly Father, I give You thanks for giving me *"...clean hands and a pure heart,..."* (Psalms 24:4) so that I can come before You boldly to pray, partnering with our Chief Intercessor. Touch the hearts of those who need to be in intercession with us on behalf of Your will to be accomplished in the earth today. In Jesus' name. Amen!

~ 10 ~
Prayers for the Prayer Room

After an experience of praying through the seven churches of Asia Minor (Turkey), I am convinced that praying the will of God, as revealed in Revelation 2 and 3, will bless your church. Pray from the perspective of the Word spoken to each of these churches: *"He who has an ear, let him hear what the Spirit says to the churches."* 94[ ]

When you pray through the prayers below, hopefully it will help you in praying for your own church to possess these godly attributes—moving her closer to "Her Glorious Destiny."

- Pray your church will be loving, not loveless. (Revelation 2:1-7)
- Pray your church will stand in the face of persecution, not shrink back. (Revelation 2:8-11)
- Pray your church will walk with integrity, not compromising. (Revelation 2:12-17)
- Pray your church will be righteous, not corrupt. (Revelation 2:18-29)
- Pray your church will be alive, not dead. (Revelation 3:1-6)
- Pray your church will be faithful, not disobedient. (Revelation 3:7-13)
- Pray your church will be passionate, not lukewarm. (Revelation 3:14-22)

Pray for the Worship Service:

Pray the Holy Spirit will convict hearts so that He may sanctify and cleanse each person in the worship service with the washing of water through the preached Word. Pray that He might present each person to Himself, a glorious church, not having spot or blemish. While in the Prayer Room, intercessors or people of prayer should be sensitive to the Holy Spirit to petition the Lord on behalf of those ministering and those seated in the pews.

Prayer Protocol:

The following is a prayer protocol that covers the five areas of the worship service. These areas are used by the Lord to bring people to Himself: 1) welcome; 2) worship; 3) Word; 4) witness; and 5) workers.

Each church should have a prayer protocol, similar to this one, established by the Senior Leader, the Prayer Pastor, or the designee for the Prayer Room. Be trained and familiar with the prayer protocol prior to praying in the Prayer Room.

Always pray the Word for each element of the worship service. Keep in mind, God's Word should always be used as our guiding Light for intercessory prayer. *"Your word is a lamp to my feet and a light to my path."* 95[ ]

1) Welcome:

A welcoming church is a warm church. Start praying before you leave home for the ministries who will be seen first by those arriving for the worship service. Pray each church attendee will feel welcomed. *"…with loving-kindness I have drawn you."* 96[ ] Know it is the Spirit who has drawn them as He did you.

If your church has a parking lot ministry, this is the first ministry that people see. It is also the first opportunity to welcome and release God's blessing over them. Pray for those in the parking lot ministry, especially during inclement weather, that they would be warm and inviting to those arriving. Also, pray for the greeters and ushers as they welcome people into your building and the Sanctuary.

Even when I am not on duty in the Prayer Room, I have made it a practice to start praying Saturday and while I'm preparing for church on Sunday morning for the church attendees, that they would feel welcomed. People should always feel welcomed whenever they enter into the House of the Lord.

2) Worship:

Praise teams and praise dancers prepare and lead the congregation into the presence of God. Pray the worship is so high the glory of God will fill the Sanctuary. Know the various elements involved in worship as it applies to the church and pray for them. Keep in mind, the Father is seeking those to worship Him *"...in spirit and in truth;..."* 97[ ] Therefore, we should come prepared to worship Him with all our hearts.

Worshippers are the beacon that draws one into the presence of the Lord. Whenever the heart of the worshipper is prepared in advance to lead worship, we are drawn to the spiritual Light of His presence as moths are drawn to the natural light. Pray for the worshippers to be prepared with clean hands and a pure heart so the Lord can use them mightily in drawing people to Himself.

Worshippers also prepare the hearts of the people to hear and receive the Word. Pray for the worshippers to go forth plowing the ground and preparing the soil of the heart for the Word that will follow.

An important part of worship and coming before the Lord is to *"...bring an offering..."* 98[ ] our first fruits and tithes. Pray for the offering and that it would be given out of a pure heart, *"...for God loves a cheerful giver."* 99[ ]

3) Word:

The Word of God is powerful. He promises that *"...it shall not return to Me void, but it shall accomplish what I please..."* 100[ ] God is sending His Word to the hearts of men to save, heal, deliver, and set free. *"Your word is a lamp to my feet and a light to my path."* 101[ ] *"Your word I have hidden in my heart, that I might not sin against You."* 102[ ] *"The entrance of Your words gives light; it gives understanding to the simple."* 103[ ] Pray that the preaching of the Word is *"...not with persuasive words of human wisdom, but in demonstration of the Spirit and of power, that your faith should not be in the wisdom of men but in the power of God."* 104[ ]

4) Witness:

In the Prayer Room we are praying for the ones the Lord has brought to church. Pray they will respond to the Word as it is ministered from the "welcome" to the "Word!" *"Behold, I stand at the door and knock."* 105[ ] *"...and you shall be witnesses to Me..."* 106[ ]

5) Workers:

When I say workers, I am not only talking about the paid staff. Pray for the volunteers who serve, including those administrators who will take the information from the ones who responded to the altar call. We are calling for prayers for all who labor amongst us. We are to know them and, when possible, call them by name. Pray the Father will meet every need they and their families might have.

Pray for a community response. Pray that those who respond to the Word will be discipled so they will become "fishers of men" and workers in their giftings in the church. Pray that they will attend a Newcomer's Class to be prepared for the harvest of souls. *"The harvest truly is plentiful..."* 107[ ] *"...for the people had a mind to work."* 108[ ]

Pray for Those Responding:

Pray that enough space is available in the Prayer Room after the altar call or invitation is given. *"The spirit indeed is willing, but the flesh is weak."* 109[ ] *"Therefore pray the Lord of the harvest..."* 110[ ] He may be calling you to pray for the harvest of souls. In the event there is an overflow in the Prayer Room, areas should be designated in advance and each person aware of the extra rooms so that there is no confusion.

It is okay to ask the person what they want prayer for. Use discernment. Ask the Lord if you are to be part of this great powerful force of His.

"Ask, and it will be given to you;..." 111[ ] *"Yet you do not have because you do not ask."* 112[ ] *"If any of you lacks wisdom, let him ask of God,..."* 113[ ]

Ask the Lord for a Scripture from His Word that the person you are praying for can stand on—His promise for them right where they are. *"The entrance of Your words gives light; it gives understanding to the simple."* 114[ ] *"Your kingdom come. Your will be done on earth as it is in heaven."* 115[ ] *"He who has an ear, let him hear what the Spirit says to the churches."* 116[ ]

Morning Prayer or Prior to Attending Your Prayer Group:

Morning prayer is part of the preparation for the Prayer Room ministry. Pray for the welcoming presence of the Holy Spirit into your church during your morning prayer time. This experience starts prior to entering the Prayer Room. The morning prayer time sets the tone for the worship experience. It will be felt from the parking lot to the pulpit. It gives everyone a true sense of community.

The Lord is calling His people to the ministry of prayer. He desires to lead those with submitted and humble hearts to fulfill His will in praying your church into "Her Glorious Destiny." Amen. So be it!

Selah Moments—pause and meditate: journal personal reflections from the Lord:

____

____

____

____

Study Questions:

1. Read Revelation 2 and 3. What did you learn from God's Word spoken to each of the seven churches in Asia Minor (Turkey)?

2. Consider what your church would look like if it was loving, standing firm in the face of persecution, walking with integrity, righteous, alive, faithful, and passionate.

3. Will you pray for your church to possess these godly attributes in increasing measure moving her closer to "Her Glorious Destiny?"

4. The Lord uses the five areas of prayer protocol of a worship service to bring people to Himself: 1) welcome; 2) worship; 3) Word; 4) witness; and 5) workers. Write a prayer with a Scripture specific to your church for each of the prayer protocol areas.

5. To always use God's Word for intercessory prayer requires knowing God's Word. Are you spending time in God's Word for yourself and for others? What would be necessary (sacrifice, change...) for you to continue to grow in God's Word and intercessory prayer?

Concluding Prayer:

Heavenly Father, how wonderful is Your name in ALL the earth. Thank You for the opportunity to learn from the seven churches in Asia Minor (Turkey). I pray my church is in alignment with the Church You have called by Your name. I release Your Word covering over the workers; keep them encouraged and in health so they can meet the demands of the harvest of souls while executing the vision You have given Your visionary. In Jesus' name. Amen! To God be the glory!

THE FOURTH KEY

The Intercessor's Response

Who may ascend into the hill of the Lord? Or who may stand in His holy place? He who has clean hands and a pure heart, who has not lifted up his soul to an idol, nor swore deceitfully. He shall receive blessing from the Lord, and righteousness from the God of his salvation. **Psalms 24:3-5**

Prayer is powerful. Amelda Thomas-Jones takes you by the hand, walking you through Biblical truths of intercessory prayer. She has written a handbook of God's when, how, where, who, why and what. This is a must read for those wanting to dive into a deeper relationship with God and to understand the principles of effective prayer.

Deborah Edwards, aka Sponge, Prayer Coordinator
Vancouver, Washington

~ 11 ~
Intimate Relationship

My grandmother once told me, "Ask the Lord to search your heart. If not, you will misinterpret the Scripture to say what you want it to say to justify your actions. Ask Holy Spirit to illuminate and confess any secret sin(s). If not, you will see and hear the truth and call it a lie." *"Be diligent to present yourself approved to God, a worker who does not need to be ashamed, rightly dividing the word of truth."* 117[ ]

The Fruit of an Intimate Relationship:

Taking time to read the Word, pray, fast, and worship the Lord will build godly character. Operate in a spirit of excellence and obedience knowing *"...to obey is better than sacrifice..."* 118[ ]

Always be faithful to seek His face and not His hands. In other words, intimate relationship with the Lord will keep you from constantly begging. It brings you to the level of confidence knowing whatever you ask in His name and according to His will, He will grant you.

Intimate relationship with the Lord can build your self-esteem. *"... when my heart is overwhelmed; lead me to the rock that is higher than I."* 119[ ]

Intimate relationship will cause you to walk with a repentant heart. I cannot tell you the number of times I cry out to Him for help. No, our intimate relationship with the Lord will not keep us from sometimes feeling sad or hoping we could circumvent trouble or sickness. It does, however, cause me to run to the Lord; to call upon Him. It causes me to be compassionate to others. And His love for me allows me to love others, *"...for love will cover a multitude of sins."* 120[ ]

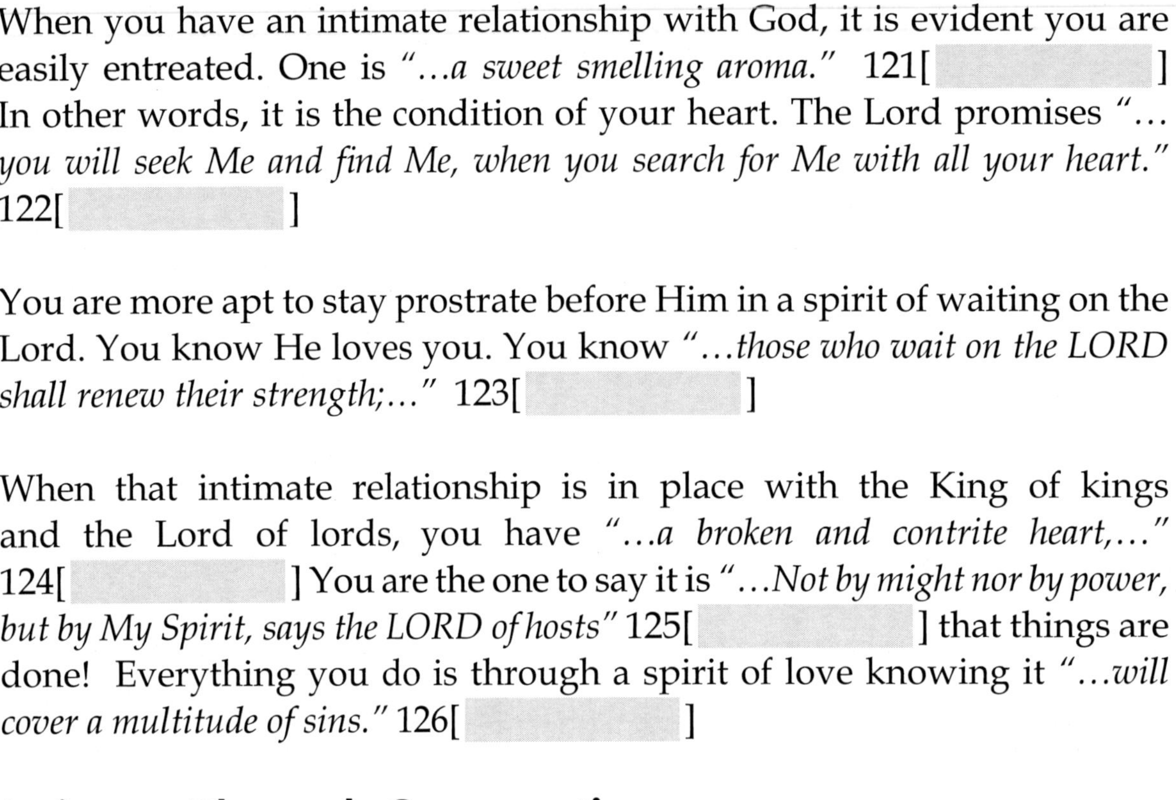

When you have an intimate relationship with God, it is evident you are easily entreated. One is *"...a sweet smelling aroma."* 121[ ] In other words, it is the condition of your heart. The Lord promises *"... you will seek Me and find Me, when you search for Me with all your heart."* 122[ ]

You are more apt to stay prostrate before Him in a spirit of waiting on the Lord. You know He loves you. You know *"...those who wait on the LORD shall renew their strength;..."* 123[ ]

When that intimate relationship is in place with the King of kings and the Lord of lords, you have *"...a broken and contrite heart,..."* 124[ ] You are the one to say it is *"...Not by might nor by power, but by My Spirit, says the LORD of hosts"* 125[ ] that things are done! Everything you do is through a spirit of love knowing it *"...will cover a multitude of sins."* 126[ ]

Intimacy Through Consecration:

I have overcome numerous adversities through prayer and fasting. Things of the flesh are removed from the Church, as well as from individuals who live a consecrated life. And it is a consecrated life that has created more room for the life of Christ to dwell—producing greater intimacy with Him.

A life of fasting and consecration before the Lord was a way of life for my grandmother. Now, after all these years, I find myself praying the same prayers she prayed: *"Purge me with hyssop, and I shall be clean; wash me, and I shall be whiter than snow."* 127[ ] *"Hide Your face from my sins, and blot out all my iniquities."* 128[ ] *"Then I will teach transgressors Your ways, and sinners shall be converted to You."* 129[ ]

You cannot be an intercessor and be moody. Consecration takes care of all of that. I recall once the Lord told me, "AMELDA, I have not called you to lock yourself away from people. You do that because you do not want to have anything to do with them."

I am a runner, one who will hide and stay by myself. The devil knows that. That is when the Holy Spirit will enter my consecrated heart. He will step in knowing I'm weak. He will whisper to me in that *"...still small voice"* 130[ ]; encouraging fellowship and *"...not forsaking the assembling of ourselves together,..."* 131[ ] His strength comes through the reassurance that He *"...is able to keep you from stumbling, and present you faultless before the presence of His glory..."* 132[ ]; *"...Who alone is wise,..."* 133[ ]

Intimacy Through Repentance:

Intercessors and people of prayer must lead a life of repentance to experience intimacy with the Lord. I have had several defining moments when the Lord God Almighty had to bring me up before Him in a spirit of repentance. That is what an intimate relationship with Him will do for you. That is what a consecrated life will bring you. Waiting in His presence will remove the dross from you!

To build an intimate relationship with the Lord, study Psalms 51. Highlight the verses that speak to you and have the Holy Spirit come with a time of refreshing to heal you. I have done this and it has brought me the balm of Gilead to heal me from sins, disappointments, and the hurts of man. He will do the same for you.

I still practice Selah moments in this Psalm. This is a start; you also will find the Word that will bring you the healing and soothing balm! For each of us there will come a time when we will say to the Lord: *"Have mercy upon me, O God, according to Your lovingkindness; according to the multitude of Your tender mercies, blot out my transgressions. Wash me thoroughly from my iniquity, and cleanse me from my sin."* (Psalms 51:1-2)

If you have not experienced this yet—live long enough and you will cry out: *"For I acknowledge my transgressions, and my sin is always before me."* (Psalms 51:3)

Knowing it is against Him alone you have sinned: *"Against You, You only, have I sinned, and done this evil in Your sight – that You may be found just when You speak, and blameless when You judge. Behold, I was brought forth in iniquity, and in sin my mother conceived me. Behold, You desire truth in the inward parts, and in the hidden part You will make me to know wisdom."* (Psalms 51:4-6)

Your cry for spiritual cleansing will come from the Lord: *"Purge me with hyssop, and I shall be clean; wash me, and I shall be whiter than snow. Make me hear joy and gladness, that the bones You have broken may rejoice. Hide Your face from my sins, and blot out all my iniquities."* (Psalms 51:7-9)

I cannot tell you how many times I have had to say: *"Create in me a clean heart, O God, and renew a steadfast spirit within me. Do not cast me away from Your presence, and do not take Your Holy Spirit from me. Restore to me the joy of Your salvation, and uphold me by Your generous Spirit. Then I will teach transgressors Your ways, and sinners shall be converted to You."* (Psalms 51:10-13)

In my hurt and wanting revenge, I have had to remember there is purpose and destiny on my life. Then I had to say: *"Deliver me from the guilt of bloodshed, O God, the God of my salvation, and my tongue shall sing aloud of Your righteousness. O Lord, open my lips, and my mouth shall show forth Your praise. For You do not desire sacrifice, or else I would give it; You do not delight in burnt offering. The sacrifices of God are a broken spirit, a broken and a contrite heart – these, O God, You will not despise. Do good in Your good pleasure to Zion; build the walls of Jerusalem. Then You shall be pleased with the sacrifices of righteousness, with burnt offering and whole burnt offering; then they shall offer bulls on Your altar."* (Psalms 51:14-19)

Intimacy Through Fasting:

Do not think fasting and dieting are the same. It does not work. The fasting I am talking about is the one Jesus completed before His ministry started. Be prepared. With that type of fast, the first thing you will encounter is the devil. He will use the Word like he did with Jesus. Be prepared to respond like Jesus did. He used the Word. Jesus was and still is the Word. Stay in and connected to the Word. Jesus is the Word you will remain connected with. *"I am the true vine, and My Father is the vinedresser."* 134[ ]

There are various fasts described throughout the Bible. Choose the one that best suits you. The one you choose is left up to you and the Lord. No matter which one you choose, if you follow its precepts, then you will have success. In my opinion, there are two types of fasts: one that pleases the flesh; and one that pleases God. Which fast will you choose? The fast that pleases man is Isaiah 58:2-5; the fast that pleases God is Isaiah 58:6-12.

I have experienced both types of fasts. Yet the fasting that pleases God is the one that brought me peace of mind, something money or possessions cannot give. In pleasing God, you can pray the Church into "Her Glorious Destiny" unencumbered.

You are the Church He will cleanse and sanctify because He loves you. He is making us holy *"...because it is written, 'Be holy, for I am holy.'"* 135[ ] We become holy only through repentance and consecration; and this is the pathway to intimacy. God so desires His people to know Him intimately so they will pray His heart.

Know that it is not the abundance of words you pray that validates your prayer before God, nor your tone of voice. It is through the condition of the heart or sincerity of your heart that your mouth will speak. *"For out of the abundance of the heart his mouth speaks."* 136[ ] Keep in mind that *"...man looks at the outward appearance, but the Lord looks at the heart."* 137[ ]

The Lord reveals His heart to those in intimate relationship with Him. The closer and more intimate we become, the more He reveals Himself. It is through consecration, repentance, and fasting that we *"Draw near to God and He will draw near to you."* 138[ ] It is out of this place of nearness with the Lord comes the intimate prayers like David prayed: Holy Father, *"As the deer pants for the water brooks, so pants my soul for You,*

O God." 139[ ] *"...in Your presence is fullness of joy; at Your right hand are pleasures forevermore."* 140[ ]

Invest in your intimate relationship with the Lord; it has eternal rewards.

Selah Moments—pause and meditate: journal personal reflections from the Lord:

____

____

____

____

Study Questions:

1. *"Be diligent to present yourself approved to God, a worker who does not need to be ashamed, rightly dividing the word of truth."* What does living this Scripture from 2 Timothy 2:15 look like in your life?

2. Have you asked the Lord to search your heart? It is a question asked multiple times through this study, but the importance is so great it is worth repeating again. From 1 Samuel 16:7 we learn, *"...man looks at the outward appearance, but the Lord looks at the heart."* What is He seeing when He looks deep into the condition of your heart? Is there anything you need to confess, change...?

3. An intimate relationship with the Lord includes taking the time to read the Word, pray, fast, and worship the Lord. Spend time asking the Lord to give you a true reflection of where you have room for growth in your relationship with Him. Share a step you will take over the next few weeks.

4. What type of fruit is evident in a person with an intimate relationship with the Lord?

5. In any relationship, if someone was always begging, the relationship would not be as full, or as beautiful, as it could potentially be. How do you purposefully seek God's face and not His hands?

6. Read Psalms 51. List the verses that the Holy Spirit uses to speak to you. Use that verse to pray back to the Lord.

7. Fasting that pleases God is found in Isaiah 58:6-12. How will you apply fasting that pleases God in your life?

8. How are you investing in an intimate relationship with the Lord?

Concluding Prayer:

Holy Heavenly Father, how excellent is Your name in the entire world. Thank You for the deepening of my intimate relationship with You during these last few weeks. You have tried me and You know my heart. Thank You for working on me from the inside out. I bless You for the Holy Spirit speaking to me through Your Word. Endeavoring to be a reflection of Your love is my heart's cry. In Jesus' name. Amen!

~ 12 ~
Covenant Relationship

We serve a covenant keeping God. If we are to fulfill our calling to pray the Church into "Her Glorious Destiny," we need to understand and enter into a covenant relationship with Him. We must also pass down these covenant principles to the generations to come so they, too, can fulfill their call to pray forth God's vision.

A covenant is an agreement between you and another. According to the Thesaurus, covenant means: Agreement; Contract; Treaty; Promise; Pledge; between two or more parties.

The covenant relationship with God and the visionary of your church will bring you into harmony with your Creator and His vision for your church. Ask the Father to reveal to you the matriarch or patriarch from Scripture that best exemplifies your covenant relationship with Him and with your church. He will. *"Ask, and it will be given to you;..."* 141[ ]

Abraham's Example:

The Lord gave me Abraham as an example of covenant relationship because of my own shortcomings. Yet, His love has redeemed me so I could leave this book as a legacy.

Abraham's covenant relationship with God was imperative for him in becoming the "father of many nations." The generations need to know the forgiveness and love of God through covenant relationship so they, too, can pray the Church into "Her Glorious Destiny."

The story of Abraham illustrates God's dedication to him through their covenant relationship. In spite of lying about Sarah being his sister and sleeping with Hagar, God forgave him and used him mightily. He will use you also! Let Him.

Abraham's Faith:

Abraham had complete confidence in God through his covenant relationship with Him. He obeyed God and took Isaac to Mount Moriah and knew God as Jehovah, his Provider. God saved Abraham's family member, Lot, and he knew God to be *"...mighty to save."* 142[ ] It was through trust in God and obedience to Him that Abraham became *"...fully convinced that what He had promised He was also able to perform."* 143[ ] And Abraham's faith in his covenant partner, God Himself, was *"...accounted to him for righteousness."* 144[ ]

Covenant with God:

Covenant is established through relationship. The first covenant relationship is with God, then with each other. Our covenant with God is indefinite. He will never break His covenant or relationship with us. We are the ones who will walk away from Him. Yet, if we will repent and *"...confess our sins, He is faithful and just to forgive us our sins and to cleanse us from all unrighteousness."* 145[ ]

Each of us should have the peace of God in our relationship with the Lord and each other. It is only through the covenant we have with God that we can experience a successful and victorious covenant with each other.

Covenant with Others:

Our covenant with each other should operate similarly to the one we have with God. We must forgive *"...one another, even as God in Christ forgave you."* 146[ ] In covenant relationship we can agree to disagree, without being disrespectful and stop speaking to each other. When in disagreement, be open to come together so that an offense will not occur and split the relationship.

Some agreements between each other are seasonal. *"To everything there is a season,..."* 147[ ] Now the type of covenant you enter into can be for a period of time, or it can be indefinite. However, this should be agreed to between all those concerned.

God's Promises and Provision:

Abraham's journey with God was a wonderful one—so should our journey be with God. God provided for him because of his obedience. Two things God gave to Abraham even with his shortcomings: His promises and His provision. What God did for Abraham, He will do for you and me. You can be a recipient of His grace just like Abraham. God has "promises and provision" for you. Jesus paid your price on the Cross. Thank God for His grace! He will cut a covenant with you. And as you covenant with others, His promises are yes and amen!

Walk in covenant integrity. That is doing the right thing when you think no one is looking. Keep in mind God sees, hears, and knows everything you are doing! Abraham was found faithful in his covenant relationship with God and man. He received the promise. *"By faith Abraham obeyed when he was called to go out to the place which he would receive as an inheritance."* 148[ ]

Through my covenant relationship with God and others, I have been empowered to experience His promises and provision, in the true sense of the word. You can also; God is no respecter of persons. With a broken and contrite heart before God, we can also receive His promises and be sustained by His provision.

It is through our covenant relationship with God and each other that we begin to experience the promise of Jesus' heart—a Bride not having spot or wrinkle, holy and without blemish—a church living and moving closer and closer to "Her Glorious Destiny."

Selah Moments – pause and meditate: journal personal reflections from the Lord:

____

____

____

____

Study Questions:

1. Who are you purposefully passing down God's covenant principles to so they, too, can fulfill their call to pray forth God's vision? List them by name.

2. Which matriarch or patriarch from Scripture has God revealed to you that best exemplifies your covenant relationship with Him and with your church?

3. What is there about that matriarch or patriarch's life that reveals your covenant relationship?

4. In spite of the sins in Abraham's life, his faith in His covenant partner, God Himself, was "*...accounted to him for righteousness.*" (Romans 4:22) Have you entered into a covenant relationship with God allowing His forgiveness to fully cover your sins so you can live on in faith? How has that covenant relationship changed your life?

5. God sees, hears, and knows everything. Covenant integrity calls for doing the right thing even when we think no one is looking. How are you doing representing the Lord even when you think no one is watching? Is there anything you need to change or make right?

6. Are you now ready to formalize your covenant relationship? Refer to "Appendix E" for instructions on how this can be done.

Concluding Prayer:

Heavenly Father, I bow in thanksgiving and praise to Your majesty in the exalted name of Jesus Christ. Thank You for the finished work of the Cross. Jesus paid the ultimate price for my covenant relationship with You. Forgive me of all secret sin(s). Thank You for the biblical matriarchs and patriarchs who, with flesh on, have inspired me to walk in covenant integrity as I collaborate with the Holy Spirit daily, as a living Epistle, praying in agreement with the visionary You have placed in my life. In Jesus' name. Amen!

~ 13 ~
Identity in Christ

I cannot tell you the amount of times as a teenager my grandmother told me to get my self-worth from the Lord. She would say to me, "AMELDA, go and search the Word and tell me who the Lord says you are. Your life is hidden in Jesus Christ," she would say. I have done this with my own children. Try it for yourself.

Today, I continue to find who I am in Him. Find out who you are in Him.

When I found the word "BELOVED" in the Bible, I fell in love for the first time in my life. You, too, are His beloved; receive His affection for you:

- *"The beloved of the LORD shall dwell in safety by Him."* 149[ ]
- *"...for so He gives His beloved sleep."* 150[ ]
- *"At the beginning of your supplications the command went out, and I have come to tell you, for you are greatly beloved:..."* 151[ ]
- *"...This is My beloved Son, in whom I am well pleased."* 152[ ]
- *"...He made us accepted in the Beloved."* 153[ ]
- *"I am my beloved's, and my beloved is mine."* 154[ ]
- *"...Beloved, I pray that you may prosper in all things and be in health, just as your soul prospers."* 155[ ]

The Bible has so much to say about who we are in Christ. Gaining our identity from Christ is especially valuable for those who have had the tendency to be a "man pleaser." A "man pleaser" is one who seeks their self-worth from mankind, or one who makes wrong decisions, or gets involved with the wrong people in order to be affirmed. Beloved, you are already accepted in the Beloved.

Get your identity and affirmation from the Lord. Men will deceive you! Those of us who get our identity from Him will not fight identity depression or suffer from low self-esteem!

Who the Lord says that I am is answered in His Word, the Bible. This is what I choose to base my identity. Your life and mine is hidden in Jesus Christ. If you are like me, you want to know what the Bible has to say about who I am:

- I am a child of God: *"But as many as received Him, to them He gave the right to become children of God,..."* 156[ ]
- I am a friend of Jesus Christ: He said, *"...I have called you friends,..."* 157[ ]
- I am a *"...treasure in earthen vessels,..."* 158[ ]
- I am a *"...pearl of great price,..."* 159[ ]
- I am the Lord's: *"...do you not know...you are not your own? For you were bought at a price..."* 160[ ]
- I am part of a *"...royal priesthood,..."* 161[ ]
- I am a member of Christ's body: *"Now you are the body of Christ, and members individually."* 162[ ]
- I am redeemed and forgiven of all my sins: *"He has delivered us from the power of darkness and conveyed us into the kingdom of the Son of His love, in whom we have redemption through His blood, the forgiveness of sins."* 163[ ]
- I am made in the image of God: *"Then God said, 'Let Us make man in Our image, according to Our likeness; let them have dominion over the fish of the sea, over the birds of the air, and over the cattle, over all the earth and over every creeping thing that creeps on the earth.' So God created man in His own image; in the image of God He created him; male and female He created them."* 164[ ]
- I am complete in Christ: *"...you are complete in Him, who is the head of all principality and power."* 165[ ]

Beloved, I would like to take this opportunity and encourage you in your most holy faith. Build yourself up praying in the Spirit. Take the Scriptural nuggets the Lord has had me share with you as a building block. This is all about you and who God says you are. Now build upon it. This foundational interaction between you and the Father is of the utmost importance. It is all in reference to how you see yourself: who you are and Whose you are.

Please know you are the Lord's *"...pearl of great price,..."* 166[ ] He sold everything by giving up His life to purchase you. You are that important to Him. You are now accepted into the Beloved! Receive and live this truth—for His glory and for your glorious destiny as part of His Bride, the Church. Amen!

Selah Moments—pause and meditate: journal personal reflections from the Lord:

____

____

____

____

Study Questions:

1. Who does the Lord say you are? You may want to write out several statements that begin with "I am"...

2. Now meditate on those truths.

3. Follow the truth of God's Word and keep them in a place that you can refer to them from time to time. You may find this a helpful strategy for coming alongside others in the future as well.

4. What is the source of your confidence that your identity is in Christ?

5. List ways you constantly reinforce your identity in Christ.

6. Are you resting in the Lord? What does that look like?

7. Write out some of the creative ways you can help others experience the rest of the Lord.

Concluding Prayer:

Heavenly Father, thank You for the Holy Spirit showing me my identity in You and leading me into Your rest. Help me to always have praises in my heart as I meditate and share Your truths about who You say I am. Thank You, my life is hidden in Jesus Christ. Give me opportunity to share with others as the Holy Spirit leads and guides me. In Jesus' name. Amen!

~ 14 ~
Authority in Christ

Power in the Name of Jesus:

For everything there is a season. This is the season of empowering ourselves in Jesus' name through the Word of God. This will enable us to stand in these last and evil days. *"Your word I have hidden in my heart, that I might not sin against You."* 167[ ]

God help us if we are found to be powerless. The sons of Sceva tried to use the name of Jesus without the power. The demons knew they did not know what they were talking about. As you are praying your church into "Her Glorious Destiny," pray with power so you don't end up like the sons of Sceva: *"...Jesus I know, and Paul I know; but who are you?"* 168[ ]

The only way we can know the power in the name of Jesus is to nurture ourselves with the spiritual food of His Word. Let us grow *"...from glory to glory, just as by the Spirit of the Lord."* 169[ ] *"And let us not grow weary while doing good,..."* 170[ ] This is achieved by eating and meditating on God's Word on a continuous basis; being *"...diligent to present yourself approved to God,...rightly dividing the word of truth."* 171[ ]

The Bible says: *"The name of the LORD is a strong tower; the righteous run to it and are safe."* 172[ ] There is power at the mention of the name of Jesus: *"...that at the name of Jesus every knee should bow,...and that every tongue should confess that Jesus Christ is Lord,..."* 173[ ]

We must have and maintain an intimate relationship with the Lord. In the natural we eat three times a day, and we snack just as often. The same is true with our relationship with the Lord. In order for us to know and experience the power in the name of Jesus, we must be feeding ourselves with the food of God's Word.

Pray in the Name of Jesus:

"And in that day you will ask Me nothing. Most assuredly, I say to you, whatever you ask the Father in My name He will give you." 174[ ] Jesus said for us to pray to the Father in His name and He would do whatever we ask. This promise is tied to Jesus' confession in the Garden when He prayed, *"...take this cup away from Me; nevertheless not My will, but Yours, be done."* 175[ ] The power to receive our answer to prayer is found in praying according to the will and Word of God.

Ministry of the Holy Spirit:

Jesus promised that *"...you shall receive power when the Holy Spirit has come upon you; and you shall be witnesses to Me..."* 176[ ] And it is the Holy Spirit who *"...will teach you all things, and bring to your remembrance all things that I said to you,..."* 177[ ] It is also the Holy Spirit who *"...will guide you into all truth;..."* 178[ ] Know that you know that God is able to keep you *"...from stumbling, and to present you faultless before the presence of His glory with exceeding joy,..."* 179[ ]

Never Stop Contending:

Because of our spiritual nourishment in the Word of God and our intimate relationship with Jesus, we are able to: experience power in His name; confidently pray in His name; and release the ministry of the Holy Spirit.

We are now equipped to pray our church into "Her Glorious Destiny."

Keep in mind as you pray, the Lord has three possible answers: yes, no, or wait. "Yes" will bring Him glory as you show and testify to His glory. When He says "no" to your request, you know from your spiritual nutrition in His Word that He has something better for you. I have experienced this for myself and I know from experience. In waiting on the Lord, we are guaranteed He will not leave us without comfort during our time of waiting.

Maintain your life with God by *"...building yourselves up on your most holy faith, praying in the Holy Spirit, keep yourselves in the love of God, looking for the mercy of our Lord Jesus Christ unto eternal life."* 180[ ]

Knowing what I know, I must impart prayer into the Church. I must impart prayer into you, this generation, and generations to come—it's my destiny. It's non-negotiable. I will teach should the Lord tarry. This is my mandate from the Lord: to equip you in praying your church into "Her Glorious Destiny." In Jesus' name.

Selah Moments—pause and meditate: journal personal reflections from the Lord:

____

____

____

____

Study Questions:

1. How are you using this season for empowering yourself in Jesus' name through the Word of God so that you can stand in these last and evil days?

2. What does it mean to pray with power in the name of Jesus?

3. How will you maintain an intimate relationship with the Lord so that you can experience power in the name of Jesus?

4. Describe a time when you have called on the Word of God for power. What would be necessary to have His power growing ever stronger in your life?

5. What are Jesus' promises regarding the Holy Spirit?

6. The Lord answers prayers with yes, no, or wait. Give a brief description as to why and how God might use each of these three responses in your life.

7. Will you join in praying your church into "Her Glorious Destiny?"

8. How does your life look different after reading God's Word and His call to pray your church into "Her Glorious Destiny?"

9. You may be a member of a local church; home church; on-line church; TV church; etc. Would you share your testimony of how God has called you to pray for your particular type of church into "Her Glorious Destiny?"

10. If you are not a member of any church and gave your life to the Lord due to your experience with this study, would you share your story?

11. Using your own words, define through Scripture how your identity is secure in Christ.

12. Based on your previous response, how might the Holy Spirit use you to disciple someone else in defining their identity in Christ?

Concluding Prayer:

Heavenly Father, I love and adore You. Thank You for the finished work of the Cross; justifying me by faith and finding my identity hidden exclusively in the finished work of the Cross. I know it is not about the wooden beams of the cross, but what Jesus did on it for me: *"…while we were still sinners, Christ died for us."* (Romans 5:8) Father, thank You for the Holy Spirit leading me into the truth of Your Word in this study of **"The Ancient Keys of Intercession."** In Jesus' name. Amen!

~ 15 ~
Stand Purposeful and Pray

Intercessors and people of prayer: this is to be your finest moment. Now is the time to stand and pray in the full assurance of God's Word and His calling upon your life. The definition of purposeful is an intention or plan; a reason for action (see Galatians 4:18). The Holy Spirit is our: director; encourager; sustainer; while we are standing in prayer!

I will share twelve truths from God's Word. The number twelve is the number of His first disciples, which now you are one. The word "stand" means to "hold our ground." Whenever we pray, it attracts resistance from the enemy. Consequently, as intercessors and people of prayer, we must take our rightful position to "stand" in Christ and collaborate with Him through the Holy Spirit. This is how we are to participate with God in seeing His *"...will be done on earth as it is in heaven."* 181[ ]

1. Stand Purposeful in God's Power:

Pray for God's power to stand and pray, regardless of the circumstances you encounter. As long as your heart is turned toward God in childlike trust, Holy Spirit, will empower you to complete the work to which He has called you.

"And He said to me, 'My grace is sufficient for you, for My strength is made perfect in weakness.' Therefore most gladly I will rather boast in my infirmities, that the power of Christ may rest upon me." (2 Corinthians 12:9)

"Finally, my brethren, be strong in the Lord and in the power of His might." (Ephesians 6:10)

"... and what is the exceeding greatness of His power toward us who believe, according to the working of His mighty power which He worked in Christ when

He raised Him from the dead and seated Him at His right hand in the heavenly places, far above all principality and power and might and dominion, and every name that is named, not only in this age but also in that which is to come." (Ephesians 1:19-20)

"For God has not given us a spirit of fear, but of power and of love and of a sound mind." 182[ ]

Do not despise the day of small things of your prayer group. Remain faithful to God's call and see how He chooses to fulfill it. *"Moreover the word of the Lord came to me, saying: 'The hands of Zerubbabel have laid the foundation of this temple; His hands shall also finish it. Then you will know that the Lord of hosts has sent Me to you. For who has despised the day of small things'"* (Zechariah 4:8-10)

Add more Scriptures from your own studies that could be prayed, read, or shared for this particular truth.

2. Stand Purposeful in God's Vision:

Pray for God's vision to be clear and always in focus.

"Then the Lord answered me and said: 'Write the vision and make it plain on tablets, that he may run who reads it.'" 183[ ]

"Stand therefore, having girded your waist with truth, having put on the breastplate of righteousness,…" (Ephesians 6:14)

"…if My people who are called by My name will humble themselves, and pray and seek My face, and turn from their wicked ways, then I will hear from heaven, and will forgive their sin and heal their land. Now My eyes will be open and My ears attentive to prayer made in this place. For now I have chosen and sanctified this house, that My name may be there forever; and My eyes and My heart will be there perpetually." (2 Chronicles 7:14-16)

Remember, God knows everything. Our responsibility is to pray. *"For I know the thoughts that I think toward you, says the Lord, thoughts of peace and not of evil, to give you a future and a hope. Then you will call upon Me and go and pray to Me, and I will listen to you. And you will seek Me and find Me, when you search for Me with all your heart.* (Jeremiah 29:11-13)

Regardless of who you are and where you are, God's will is for you to *"Rejoice always, pray without ceasing, in everything give thanks; for this is the will of God in Christ Jesus for you."* 184[ ]

Add more Scriptures from your own studies that could be prayed, read, or shared for this particular truth.

3. Stand Purposeful in the Person of the Holy Spirit:

Pray for the Holy Spirit to empower you to pray the heart of the Father. Whatever vision God has placed in your heart, the Holy Spirit will be faithful to inspire and direct your prayers.

"...'Not by might nor by power, but by My Spirit,' says the Lord of hosts." (Zechariah 4:6)

"And I will pray the Father, and He shall give you another Comforter, that He may abide with you forever;..." (John 14:16)

"Likewise the Spirit also helps in our weaknesses. For we do not know what we should pray for as we ought, but the Spirit Himself makes intercession for us with groanings which cannot be uttered. Now He who searches the hearts knows what the mind of the Spirit is, because He makes intercession for the saints according to the will of God." (Romans 8:26-27)

The Holy Spirit has a purpose; He will bring back God's vision when you are feeling defeated. *"But the Helper, the Holy Spirit, whom the Father will send in My name, He will teach you all things, and bring to your remembrance all things that I said to you."* 185[ ]

Add more Scriptures from your own studies that could be prayed, read, or shared for this particular truth.

4. Stand Purposeful in Thanksgiving and Praise:

Always, always, always make room for praise. Thank the Lord for what He has done. Recall God's past faithfulness and specifically name areas or ways He has been faithful and thank Him.

"Praise the Lord! Praise God in His sanctuary; praise Him in His mighty firmament! Praise Him for His mighty acts; praise Him according to His excellent greatness! Praise Him with the sound of the trumpet; praise Him with the lute and harp! Praise Him with the timbrel and dance; praise Him with stringed instruments and flutes! Praise Him with loud cymbals; praise Him with clashing cymbals! Let everything that has breath praise the Lord. Praise the Lord!" (Psalms 50)

"Sing and rejoice, O daughter of Zion! For behold, I am coming and I will dwell in your midst," says the Lord. (Zechariah 2:10)

"I will praise You, O Lord, with my whole heart; I will tell of all Your marvelous works. I will be glad and rejoice in You; I will sing praise to Your name, O Most High." (Psalms 9:1-2)

Thanksgiving and praise ushers us into the presence of God. This is where we gain the revelation of how to pray. *"Enter into His gates with thanksgiving, and into His courts with praise. Be thankful to Him, and bless His name. For the Lord is good; His mercy is everlasting, and His truth endures to all generations."* (Psalms 100:4-5)

Add more Scriptures from your own studies that could be prayed, read, or shared for this particular truth.

5. Stand Purposeful in the Cleansing Blood of the Lamb:

Spiritually and metaphorically place the blood on the door post of where the prayer group will meet and individually over the hearts of each member of the group. Pray for cleansing and the removal of all hindrances so your prayers can be powerful and effectual.

"And they shall take some of the blood and put it on the two doorposts and on the lintel of the houses ... For the Lord will pass through to strike the Egyptians; and when He sees the blood on the lintel and on the two doorposts, the Lord will pass over the door and not allow the destroyer to come into your houses to strike you." (Exodus 12:7, 23)

"Create in me a clean heart, O God, and renew a steadfast spirit within me. Do not cast me away from Your presence, and do not take Your Holy Spirit from me. Restore to me the joy of Your salvation, and uphold me by Your generous Spirit." (Psalms 51:10-12)

"Search me, O God, and know my heart; try me, and know my anxieties; and see if there is any wicked way in me, and lead me in the way everlasting." 186[ ]

"But if we walk in the light as He is in the light, we have fellowship with one another, and the blood of Jesus Christ His Son cleanses us from all sin. If we say that we have no sin, we deceive ourselves, and the truth is not in us. If we confess our sins, He is faithful and just to forgive us our sins and to cleanse us from all unrighteousness." (1 John 1:7-9)

Add more Scriptures from your own studies that could be prayed, read, or shared for this particular truth.

6. Stand Purposeful in God's Presence:

God is in the midst of your newly formed prayer group. Pray for God to illuminate your hearts through the power of the Holy Spirit so you can intercede out of His inspiration, direction, and rest.

"The Lord your God in your midst, the Mighty One, will save; He will rejoice over you with gladness, He will quiet you with His love, He will rejoice over you with singing." (Zephaniah 3:17)

"And He said, 'My Presence will go with you, and I will give you rest.'" 187[ ]

"Let your conduct be without covetousness; be content with such things as you have. For He Himself has said, 'I will never leave you nor forsake you.' So we may boldly say: 'The Lord is my helper; I will not fear. What can man do to me?'" (Hebrews 13:5-6)

"Come to Me, all you who labor and are heavy laden, and I will give you rest. Take My yoke upon you and learn from Me, for I am gentle and lowly in heart, and you will find rest for your souls. For My yoke is easy and My burden is light." (Matthew 11:28-30)

"I, therefore, the prisoner of the Lord, beseech you to walk worthy of the calling with which you were called, with all lowliness and gentleness, with longsuffering, bearing with one another in love, endeavoring to keep the unity of the Spirit in the bond of peace." (Ephesians 4:1-3)

"You will show me the path of life; in Your presence is fullness of joy; at Your right hand are pleasures forevermore." (Psalms 16:11)

Add more Scriptures from your own studies that could be prayed, read, or shared for this particular truth.

7. Stand Purposeful in the Belief of Jesus, the Christ:

Pray for an intimate, faith-filled connection with your Lord and Savior so you can prayerfully collaborate with Him, through the inspiration and direction of the Holy Spirit.

"Therefore He is also able to save to the uttermost those who come to God through Him, since He always lives to make intercession for them." (Hebrews 7:25)

"Nor is there salvation in any other, for there is no other name under heaven given among men by which we must be saved." 188[ ]

"Do you not believe that I am in the Father, and the Father in Me? The words that I speak to you I do not speak on My own authority; but the Father who dwells in Me does the works. Believe Me that I am in the Father and the Father in Me, or else believe Me for the sake of the works themselves." (John 14:10-11)

Pray with the mind of Christ. *"Let this mind be in you which was also in Christ Jesus,…"* (Philippians 2:5)

Pray in confidence. *"… being confident of this very thing, that He who has begun a good work in you will complete it until the day of Jesus Christ;…"* (Philippians 1:6-7)

"Now this is the confidence that we have in Him, that if we ask anything according to His will, He hears us. And if we know that He hears us, whatever we ask, we know that we have the petitions that we have asked of Him." (1 John 5:14-15)

Add more Scriptures from your own studies that could be prayed, read, or shared for this particular truth.

8. Stand Purposeful in the Reality There is an Enemy:

Remember we have an enemy: you are not walking in denial of your situation. Have you documented the prayer vision? Now write it and make it clear! The prayer vision will help you stay aligned with God's purpose and perspective, and not become overwhelmed by your circumstances. Pray for the prayer vision to be firmly established in your heart and that your prayers would flow out of it.

"For we wrestle not against flesh and blood, but against principalities, against powers, against the rulers of the darkness of this world, against spiritual wickedness in high places." 189[ ]

"For though we walk in the flesh, we do not war according to the flesh. For the weapons of our warfare are not carnal but mighty in God for pulling down strongholds, casting down arguments and every high thing that exalts itself against the knowledge of God, bringing every thought into captivity to the obedience of Christ,…" (2 Corinthians 10:3-5)

"The thief does not come except to steal, and to kill, and to destroy." 190[ ]

"These things I have spoken to you, that in Me you may have peace. In the world you will have tribulation; but be of good cheer, I have overcome the world." (John 16:33)

Add more Scriptures from your own studies that could be prayed, read, or shared for this particular truth.

9. Stand Purposeful in Your Authority in Christ:

Respond to God's call to pray by exercising your authority in Christ. Pray for greater understanding of the authority you possess as a follower of Christ Jesus, empowered by the Holy Spirit.

The Lord wants to encourage you; God has called you to partner with Him in prayer: *"Most assuredly, I say to you, he who believes in Me, the works that I do he will do also; and greater works than these he will do, because I go to My Father. And whatever you ask in My name, that I will do, that the Father may be glorified in the Son. If you ask anything in My name, I will do it."* (John 14:12-14)

"And He said to them, 'I saw Satan fall like lightning from heaven. Behold, I give you the authority to trample on serpents and scorpions, and over all the power of the enemy, and nothing shall by any means hurt you.'" 191[ ]

"Assuredly, I say to you, whatever you bind on earth will be bound in heaven, and whatever you loose on earth will be loosed in heaven." (Matthew 18:18)

Add more Scriptures from your own studies that could be prayed, read, or shared for this particular truth.

10. Stand Purposeful in the Finished Work of the Cross:

It is finished; *tetelestai* is the Greek word for "finished." Yes, *tetelestai* says you can partner with God in the prayer assignment He has entrusted to you. I had the same doubt when the Lord on June 24, 1977 called me to the ministry of F.A.I.T.H. He said to me, "Now I am saying to you; you have the power through the finished work of the Cross. Pray for healing: physical, emotional, spoken/yet unspoken..."

"Surely He has borne our griefs and carried our sorrows; yet we esteemed Him stricken, smitten by God, and afflicted. But He was wounded for our transgressions, He was bruised for our iniquities; the chastisement for our peace was upon Him, and by His stripes we are healed." (Isaiah 53:4-5)

"Then they cried out to the Lord in their trouble, and He saved them out of their distresses. He sent His word and healed them, and delivered them from their destructions. Oh, that men would give thanks to the Lord for His goodness, and for His wonderful works to the children of men!" (Psalms 107:19-21)

"Blessed be the God and Father of our Lord Jesus Christ, who according to His abundant mercy has begotten us again to a living hope through the resurrection of Jesus Christ from the dead,..." (1 Peter 1:3)

"Jesus said to her, 'I am the resurrection and the life. He who believes in Me, though he may die, he shall live. And whoever lives and believes in Me shall never die...'" 192[ ]

Tetelestai: the finished work of the Cross. He had to go so He could send us the Comforter. *"Nevertheless I tell you the truth. It is to your advantage that I go away; for if I do not go away, the Helper will not come to you; but if I depart, I will send Him to you."* (John 16:7)

"But you shall receive power when the Holy Spirit has come upon you; and you shall be witnesses to Me in Jerusalem, and in all Judea and Samaria, and to the end of the earth." 193[ ]

"And with great power the apostles gave witness to the resurrection of the Lord Jesus. And great grace was upon them all." (Acts 4:33)

Add more Scriptures from your own studies that could be prayed, read, or shared for this particular truth.

11. Stand Purposeful in the Divine Thirst for God:

Pray for hearts to grow closer to God and to live a life of intimacy with Him.

"As the deer pants for the water brooks, so pants my soul for You, O God. My soul thirsts for God, for the living God. When shall I come and appear before God?" 194[ ]

"On the last day, that great day of the feast, Jesus stood and cried out, saying, 'If anyone thirsts, let him come to Me and drink. He who believes in Me, as the Scripture has said, out of his heart will flow rivers of living water.' But this He spoke concerning the Spirit, whom those believing in Him would receive; for the Holy Spirit was not yet given, because Jesus was not yet glorified." (John 7:37-39)

"Jesus answered and said to her, 'Whoever drinks of this water will thirst again, but whoever drinks of the water that I shall give him will never thirst. But the water that I shall give him will become in him a fountain of water springing up into everlasting life.'" (John 4:13-14)

"Blessed are they which do hunger and thirst after righteousness: for they shall be filled." 195[ ]

Add more Scriptures from your own studies that could be prayed, read, or shared for this particular truth.

12. Stand Purposeful in Your Own God-Given Calling:

God has called you to pray—whether it is for a ministry, a school, our country, a neighbor; whatever it is, God has called you and you are to obey. Stand in the confidence of God's call on your life; follow the Holy Spirit's inspiration and direction in fulfilling this divine prayer assignment.

"Brethren, I do not count myself to have apprehended; but one thing I do, forgetting those things which are behind and reaching forward to those things which are ahead, I press toward the goal for the prize of the upward call of God in Christ Jesus." (Philippians 3:13-14)

"Let us hold fast the confession of our hope without wavering, for He who promised is faithful." (Hebrews 10:23)

"Therefore, brethren, be even more diligent to make your call and election sure, for if you do these things you will never stumble;..." (2 Peter 1:10)

"Now to Him who is able to keep you from stumbling, and to present you faultless before the presence of His glory with exceeding joy, to God our Savior, Who alone is wise, be glory and majesty, dominion and power, both now and forever. Amen." 196[ ]

Add more Scriptures from your own studies that could be prayed, read, or shared for this particular truth.

Start praying now as you partner with God to bring His Kingdom into the circumstances of this world so His will can be done.

And remember, God is with you and for you: *"The Lord bless you and keep you; the Lord make His face shine upon you, and be gracious to you; the Lord lift up His countenance upon you, and give you peace."* (Numbers 6:24-26)

Selah Moments—pause and meditate: journal personal reflections from the Lord:

____

____

____

____

Commissioning Prayer:

Holy Father, how excellent is Your name in all the earth. I, ________________ (insert your name), acknowledge that You have touched my heart, my mind, and my mouth with the task of intercessory prayer. As You called Your disciples, You now have called me to be one. Walking in Your precepts, I decree and declare, knowing there is *"...no other name under heaven...by which we must be saved."* 197[ ] Jesus is the name above all names; *"...that at the name of Jesus every knee should bow...and that every tongue should confess that Jesus Christ is Lord, to the glory of God the Father."* 198[ ]

Thank You, Holy Father, I ___________ (insert your name), accept my commission to pray Your will be done. I answered and with the help of Christ will continue to answer Your call to pray.

"Search me, O God, and know my heart; try me, and know my anxieties; and see if there is any wicked way in me, and lead me in the way everlasting." (Psalms 139:23-24)

I submit to Your will to *"...pray without ceasing, in everything give thanks;..."* (1 Thessalonians 5:17-18). I will answer and be diligent to Your call. I will pray in accordance with John 3:30 that You, Jesus, *"...must increase but I must decrease."* Help me to pray according to Sola Scriptura (Spanish for "Scripture only") in accordance to Psalms 24:4 with *"...clean hands and a pure heart..."*

I yield to the direction and empowerment of the Holy Spirit for the advancement of Your Kingdom. He will lead and guide me *"...into all truth..."* (John 16:13)

Father, thank You for the finished work of the Cross; for keeping me through the Holy Spirit which You promised and released to me to comfort, lead, guide, and direct me into all Truth. I endeavor to *"...walk by faith and not by sight."* 199[ ] And to glorify You, praying for all to be saved, healed, delivered, and set free!

Now with the full assurance of faith, I will purposefully pray boldly knowing nothing shall be able to separate me *"...from the love of God which is in Christ Jesus our Lord."* 200[ ] In the name of Jesus. Amen!

APPENDICES

~ APPENDIX A ~
Salvation

Confess With Your Mouth and Believe in Your Heart:

"But what does it say? "The word is near you, in your mouth and in your heart" (that is, the word of faith which we preach): that if you confess with your mouth the Lord Jesus and believe in your heart that God has raised Him from the dead, you will be saved. For with the heart one believes unto righteousness and with the mouth confession is made unto salvation. For the Scripture says, "Whoever believes on Him will not be put to shame." For there is no distinction between Jew and Greek, for the same Lord over all is rich to all who call upon Him. For "whoever calls on the name of the Lord shall be saved." (Romans 10:8-13)

As you believe and receive Jesus in your heart in accordance to the Scripture, you are saved. This is the beginning of a beautiful journey of growing in the knowledge and the ways of God.

God Loves You So Much:

To you who just received Jesus as your personal Savior, let me be the first to welcome you into God's Family which is also known as the Body of Christ. God loves you and now you have received a wonderful expression of His love, which is everlasting life with Him.

"For God so loved the world that He gave His only begotten Son, that whoever believes in Him should not perish but have everlasting life. For God did not send His Son into the world to condemn the world, but that the world through Him might be saved. He who believes in Him is not condemned; but he who does not believe is condemned already, because he has not believed in the name of the only begotten Son of God. And this is the condemnation, that the light has come into the world, and men loved darkness rather than light, because their deeds were evil." (John 3:16-19)

Seek Out a Christ-Centered Church:

Be sure as you visit churches to make sure they teach Jesus and Him crucified. *"…But we preach Christ crucified, to the Jews a stumbling block and to the Greeks foolishness,…"* (1 Corinthians 1:23)

I know with modern technology you can join an on-line church, a home church, or a TV church. Whatever form of church you are drawn to, make sure it is a church that teaches Jesus Christ is Lord to the glory of God the Father.

I welcome you in joining us and becoming part of this study of **"The Ancient Keys of Intercession."**

A Prayer of Thanksgiving:

Dear Father, I _______________ (insert your name), thank You for becoming my Heavenly Father. Thank You for dying for me and forgiving my sins. I praise and worship You with a heart of thanksgiving. I can now say I am a child of God because I have confessed with my mouth the Lord Jesus, and I believe in my heart that God has raised Him from the dead. Jesus Christ is my Lord and I will serve Him, from this moment on, through the inspiration and direction of the Holy Spirit. Heavenly Father, thank You for the promise of 1 John 1:9 that I can cry out to You when I sin and You are faithful and just to forgive me and to cleanse me from all my sin. Lord, I love You with all my heart and soul. In Jesus' name. Amen!

~ APPENDIX B ~
Praying Beyond the Walls

God calls us to be the Church. If you are praying your church into "Her Glorious Destiny," you are praying for things going on both inside and outside the walls of the physical church building.

It's a blessing to write this exhortation to the number of people who have approached me in the past and asked, "How do I start my own prayer ministry of praying for others?" These are people who, in addition to praying for their church and visionary, are called by God to pray for: a specific ministry; a school; a person or child; the military; your country; a team; a friend.

A typical example I hear repeatedly is: "I perceive the Lord is calling me to pray for my neighborhood; or, I want to open my home for prayer for our country; or, I am a Senior and I want to pray for the children I see playing in my neighborhood or going to school."

God desires to equip faithful intercessors and people of prayer to apply these same prayer principles set forth in this study to pray for "the Church beyond the walls." These principles are established on the truth of God's Word and are universally applicable in praying the entire Church into "Her Glorious Destiny."

Whatever the prayer burden or need the Lord has placed on your heart, the reply is the same: apply the prayer principles set forth in this study under the inspiration and direction of the Holy Spirit.

First, position yourself to communicate the burden you have, especially if you are meeting or will be praying with others. Follow the outline of the study to share these prayer principles with the members of your group. Allow the Holy Spirit to guide you as to when and how to share the specific principles. They should be done as the group matures and is ready to receive.

Prayer Principles from this Study:

- Chapter 1—Everyone is called to pray—each member of group
- Chapter 2—Foundational reasons to pray—why the group exists
- Chapter 3—To pray effectively—individually and as a group
- Chapter 4—Practical guidelines for interceding as a group
- Chapter 5—God's vision for the group (a ministry, a school)
- Chapter 6—God's visionary for the group
- Chapter 7—Leader of the group and steward of the vision
- Chapter 8—Location, time, and expectations for the group
- Chapter 9—Preparation for the group members
- Chapter 10—Specific types of prayers
- Chapter 11—Intimacy with God and unity within the group
- Chapter 12—Covenant relationships with God and the group
- Chapter 13—Individual and group identity in Christ
- Chapter 14—Your authority in Christ
- Chapter 15—Now is the time to start praying

Additional Encouragement:

- Pray, never giving up, even though we do not see the outcome. We will continue to see Jesus, comforted by the Holy Spirit!
- Someone should be able to lead and keep things moving in an orderly fashion; understand who is the leader and the responsibility of leading.
- Agree how often you will meet as a group.
- I recommend prayer time should not last more than an hour.
- And remember, you are never alone: *"The Lord bless you and keep you; the Lord make His face shine upon you, and be gracious to you; the Lord lift up His countenance upon you, and give you peace."* (Numbers 6:24-26)

A Blessing Prayer:

I give You praise, honor, glory; and I worship You, oh Lord. What a blessing it is to partner with You. Thank You for the regenerating power of the washing of the water of the Word of God. Thank You for giving us eyes to see and a heart to perceive even when we do not see You working, yet knowing You are at work on our behalf. You are our Lord and Provider, and You know the thoughts and plans You have for us.

Thank You for the guidance of the Holy Spirit in "Praying Beyond the Walls"—souls to be won, healing to be received, prison doors to be opened, and captives to be set free! Thank You for the call to pray.

Thank You for never leaving us or forsaking us. Thank You for calling us to pray anywhere, anytime, any place; helping us in the Holy Spirit to be obedient to the call.

Thank You for the blessing of this book to equip so many to approach You in prayer on behalf of others and myself. All praise, honor, and glory belongs to You. I worship and praise You through the finished "Tetelestai" work of the Cross. This amazing journey of the power of the Cross in prayer with You is just starting. Holy Spirit, I am ready for it is *"...'Not by might nor by power, but by My Spirit,' says the LORD of hosts"* (Zechariah 4:6) that answers are received. I pray all these things in the name of Jesus. Amen!

~ APPENDIX C ~
Scriptural References

Chapter 1:

1 1 Thessalonians 5:17
2 Matthew 16:18
3 Luke 18:1
4 Jeremiah 17:9
5 Acts 17:28
6 Malachi 3:10
7 2 Corinthians 9:7
8 1 Corinthians 14:40
9 James 5:16
10 2 Timothy 2:15
11 Matthew 18:20
12 Jude 3
13 John 14:13
14 John 13:34
15 Luke 11:2

Chapter 2:

16 John 16:13
17 Philippians 4:6
18 1 Samuel 30:8
19 1 Samuel 30:8
20 Numbers 23:19
21 Jeremiah 29:13
22 1 Timothy 2:8
23 Ezekiel 22:30
24 1 Timothy 2:1-2
25 2 Chronicles 7:14

Chapter 3:

26 Hebrews 12:2
27 Ephesians 4:32
28 Psalm 24:4
29 1 Samuel 16:7
30 Galatians 6:7
31 Ephesians 4:32
32 Matthew 18:8
33 Matthew 18:11
34 Matthew 18:20
35 Hebrews 7:25
36 Matthew 15:14
37 2 Peter 1:10

Chapter 4:

38 Hebrews 7:25
39 Ezekiel 22:30
40 Proverbs 18:16
41 Psalm 24:4
42 Luke 22:26
43 Matthew 18:15
44 Matthew 18:16
45 Ephesians 4:32
46 Ephesians 4:3
47 Ephesians 5:26-27
48 1 Peter 1:16
49 Ephesians 6:12
50 1 John 1:7
51 Ephesians 6:11
52 Jude 3
53 Matthew 10:19-20
54 Romans 12:10
55 Matthew 6:6
56 Psalm 91:5

Chapter 5:

57 Ephesians 5:27

Chapter 6:

58 James 5:16-18
59 Jeremiah 3:15
60 Matthew 6:10
61 1 Timothy 2:1-2
62 Proverbs 18:21
63 Deuteronomy 28:2
64 Malachi 3:10
65 Proverbs 10:22
66 Matthew 6:10
67 Philippians 4:7
68 Jeremiah 3:15
69 Isaiah 54:17
70 Psalm 16:11
71 John 4:23
72 2 Timothy 2:2
73 Acts 6:3-4

Chapter 7:

74 Matthew 6:33
75 Habakkuk 2:2
76 Habakkuk 2:3
77 Isaiah 11:2
78 Ephesians 4:3
79 Matthew 11:12
80 Nehemiah 4:17

Chapter 8:

81 1 John 4:19
82 Isaiah 55:11
83 Colossians 1:10
84 Hebrews 3:15
85 John 8:32
86 John 8:36
87 Ephesians 2:16
88 Matthew 6:10
89 Mark 16:17
90 1 John 5:14-15

Chapter 9:

91 Psalm 139:23
92 Psalm 24:4
93 Hebrews 13:5

Chapter 10:

94 Revelation 2:7
95 Psalm 119:105
96 Jeremiah 31:3
97 John 4:23
98 1 Chronicles 16:29
99 2 Corinthians 9:7
100 Isaiah 55:11
101 Psalm 119:105

102 Psalm 119:11
103 Psalm 119:130
104 1 Corinthians 2:4-5
105 Revelation 3:20
106 Acts 1:8
107 Matthew 9:37
108 Nehemiah 4:6
109 Matthew 26:41
110 Matthew 9:37
111 Matthew 7:7
112 James 4:2
113 James 1:5
114 Psalm 119:130
115 Matthew 6:10
116 Revelation 2:7

Chapter 11:

117 2 Timothy 2:15
118 1 Samuel 15:22
119 Psalm 61:2
120 1 Peter 4:8
121 Ephesians 5:2
122 Jeremiah 29:13
123 Isaiah 40:31
124 Psalm 51:17
125 Zechariah 4:6
126 1 Peter 4:8
127 Psalm 51:7
128 Psalm 51:9
129 Psalm 51:13
130 1 Kings 19:12
131 Hebrews 10:25
132 Jude 24
133 Jude 25
134 John 15:1
135 1 Peter 1:16
136 Luke 6:45
137 1 Samuel 16:7
138 James 4:8
139 Psalm 42:1
140 Psalm 16:11

Chapter 12:

141 Matthew 7:7
142 Isaiah 63:1
143 Romans 4:21
144 Romans 4:22
145 1 John 1:9
146 Ephesians 4:32
147 Ecclesiastes 3:1
148 Hebrews 11:8

Chapter 13:

149 Deuteronomy 33:12
150 Psalm 127:2
151 Daniel 9:23
152 Matthew 3:17
153 Ephesians 1:6
154 Song of Solomon 6:3
155 3 John 2
156 John 1:12
157 John 15:15
158 2 Corinthians 4:7
159 Matthew 13:46
160 I Corinthians 6:19-20
161 1 Peter 2:9
162 1 Corinthians 12:27
163 Colossians 1:13-14
164 Genesis 1:26-27
165 Colossians 2:10
166 Matthew 13:46

Chapter 14:

167 Psalm 119:11
168 Acts 19:15
169 2 Corinthians 3:18
170 Galatians 6:9
171 2 Timothy 2:15
172 Proverbs 18:10
173 Philippians 2:10-11
174 John 16:23
175 Luke 22:42
176 Acts 1:8
177 John 14:26
178 John 16:13
179 Jude 24
180 Jude 20

Chapter 15:

181 Matthew 6:10
182 2 Timothy 1:7
183 Habakkuk 2:2
184 2 Thessalonians 5:15-16
185 John 14:26
186 Psalm 139:23-24
187 Exodus 33:14
188 Acts 4:12
189 Ephesians 6:12
190 John 10:10
191 Luke 10:18-19
192 John 11:25-26
193 Acts 1:8
194 Psalm 42:1-2
195 Matthew 5:6
196 Jude 24-25
197 Acts 4:12
198 Philippians 2:10-11
199 2 Corinthians 5:7
200 Romans 8:39

~ APPENDIX D ~

Personal Prayer Journal

Awaken Your Heart:

Journaling is a means of awakening our hearts to communicate with God. It starts with positioning ourselves before God like the boy Samuel, who was instructed by Eli to say: *"Speak, LORD, for Your servant hears."* (1 Samuel 3:9)

Journaling is simply writing down what you sense you are hearing from the Lord. Don't worry about spelling or punctuation; simply write out of the flow of spontaneous thoughts that come.

Don't feel rushed; rest in the presence of God, listening for His still small voice. Also, feel the freedom to ask God clarifying questions. He truly loves the conversational interaction with His children.

Hearing God Must Be Learned:

Hearing and conversing with God is something that must be learned. Go back through what you have written and ask the Holy Spirit to confirm His words to you and attach Scriptural references to what you have written.

There is no substitute for conversing directly with God. Journaling is but one way many have found to cultivate a conversational relationship with God—to live progressively more out of the inspiration and direction of the Holy Spirit—God's intent for everyone.

Invite the Holy Spirit to Lead:

The important thing is to find God's way of communicating with you. Invite the Holy Spirit to lead you as to how He wants you to journal. Here are some suggestions to consider:

- Quiet your heart through thanksgiving and praise (praise God for Who He is and what He has done).
- Pray for God to speak to you: the prayer of Samuel.
- Pray for ears to hear what the Spirit is saying.
- Focus on one of God's attributes: His love, faithfulness, mercy, kindness...
- Write what you are sensing in your heart.
- Follow the flow of thoughts; there is a divine theme to the inspired thoughts of the Holy Spirit.
- Continue to express your thankfulness to God.
- When you sense you are done, ask God to confirm it to your heart.
- End in thanksgiving and praise.
- Finish with a prayer of protection over the seeds of truth which God planted in your heart.

A Prayer to Cultivate Greater Communication with God:

Blessed Father, thank You for being here and encouraging me to surrender my will to Yours. It is no longer I who live, but You live through me by the Holy Spirit leading and guiding me. You are the One who will keep me *"...from stumbling, and to present..."* me faultless *"...before the presence of His glory."* (Jude 24)

My beloved Father, as I cultivate a relationship with You, teach me how to quiet my heart so that I can hear Your still small voice. Call me through the leading of the Holy Spirit to commune with You. Beloved Father, as Eli instructed Samuel, I now instruct my spirit: *"Speak, LORD, for Your servant hears."* (1 Samuel 3:9)

Holy Spirit, help me to slow down to a pace that will cause me to hear the voice of my Savior speaking. Holy Spirit, help me to be obedient—having a heart of obedience as the Holy Spirit leads. In Jesus' name I pray. Amen!

~ APPENDIX E ~
Covenant

This Covenant is an agreement with a particular entity: your church; organization; ministry; prayer group; and/or person in praying your church into "Her Glorious Destiny" as an intercessor or person of prayer.

Let it be known, this book covers the various areas you will be expected to covenant in. You are further expected to search the Scriptures, under the leading of the Holy Spirit, to find the covenant God made with a biblical character that best describes you.

Fill in the blanks below:

Biblical Character: ______________________________________

Scriptural Reference: ______________________________________

Remember, a Covenant is an agreement and a promise between you and another! Should you decide to break it, follow the same protocol as when you initiated it—walk it out with integrity!

- - - - - - - - - - - - - - - - Tear along line and turn in - - - - - - - - - - - - - - - -

The "entity" that I am entering into covenant relationship with:

____

Print your name: ______________________________________

Your signature: ______________________________________

Date: ______________________________________

~ APPENDIX F ~
Testimonies

Kellie La Follette
West Linn, Oregon

During the summer of 2016, Amelda invited me into a specific role of helping draft some of the questions on this latest revision of *The Ancient Keys of Intercession.*

Had you been near, over the course of the summer, you would have heard, "Kel, stay in your lane," repeated many times over with love and tenderness. We began to joke that I drove a little red bumper car with a flag on the back which prominently displayed the word "God." It was never more than a gentle bump as Amelda helped steer me back into my lane—a lane of learning, serving, and growing in prayer.

As the summer drew to a close, an interesting thing began to happen. One day the women's ministry leader asked if I would host a time of praying for all that God had in mind for the upcoming year of women's ministry. I searched through the pages of this book, *The Ancient Keys of Intercession,* to prepare for our time together. Five of us gathered in my home asking God to lead. It was a beautiful and unique day unlike any I had ever experienced before.

Later, I was asked to officially join the women's leadership team in a new role of prayer. Shortly after that came an invitation to lead a prayer team covering a women's retreat weekend 6 months out that is part of a larger national event. Once again, I returned to the pages of *The Ancient Keys of Intercession,* which is rich in Scripture to guide our time together.

You might be able to see what appears to be a clear trail here, but you would be missing the fact that due to a mass radiation accident that burned my eyes in 2004, it is rare that I am able to leave home. I'm no longer able to go to church in the traditional sense. It would be easy to be left isolated here, but God can do truly amazing things when you ask.

So, look at the path again. God crossed my life with Amelda who lives over 2,000 miles away. We have literally been together in person only a handful of times. And yet, our Heavenly Father has used that link to grow my life in prayer, closeness to Him, and opportunities to encourage me to encourage others.

I won't be able to attend the events I am praying for. That is not what is important. What is important is knowing in the deepest part of your heart God hears prayer. He sees. He knows. He cares. Prayer matters. He prepares. He gives the tools. God is able to do more than I could have ever imagined. Think about it for a moment. Who gets invited to lead a prayer team when you can't physically attend church or the event you are praying for? How is that even possible? He is God. *"Now to him who is able to do immeasurably more than all we ask or imagine, according to his power that is at work in us, to him be glory in the church and in Christ Jesus throughout all generations forever and ever! Amen."* (Ephesians 3:20-21)

I encourage you to open the pages of this book, *The Ancient Keys of Intercession,* and know God in ways beyond anything you can currently imagine through prayer. Don't be surprised if your life and the lives of those around you are forever changed as you pray.

Thank you Amelda, Pastor Greg and Karen Fry, Jason Atkinson, Ginger McHenry, and my husband Joel. You have forever changed my life, nudging my little red bumper car into God's lane and a life of prayer.

B. Evonne Hinson
Seattle, Washington

Sister Amelda, it was a blessing to talk with you and to know God is concerned about me. I desperately needed His touch. Through prayer, He touched me. All glory goes to God and the Lord Jesus Christ for giving me this testimony. This is my story.

During the months of April through August, 2016, I was distressed and burdened with spiritual and physical issues; mostly dealing with physical and emotional residue from a medical surgery that occurred 5 years ago. The medical procedure left me legally blind; my strength and joy was being challenged, combined with spiritual persecution beyond my control. So I went to the only One who could help me. I went before the Lord Jesus Christ in a state of an emergency; I cried out to Him from the deep regions of my soul for help. I had been praying for such a long time and things seemed to be stagnant. In my prayer to God, I told Him that I no longer knew what to pray, I no longer could find the words to speak, I could only cry out from my spirit. So I asked God if He heard my cry for comfort and peace. I said, "God, You said if I draw near to You, You would draw near to me; so here I am, speak Lord." In His mercy, I asked for two things: (1) "Would You hear my cry and send someone to pray for me;" and (2) "Lord, I want to hear a word from You that is specifically for me. I am standing in faith in Christ Jesus, waiting and expecting to hear from You. In Jesus' name, Your daughter." This was my prayer for five long months. *"In my distress, I called upon the Lord, and cried out to my God; He heard my voice from His temple, and my cry came before Him, even to His ears."* (Psalms 18:6)

This is the testimony that Jesus Christ gave me. Upon returning home from travel on August 21, 2016, there was a telephone message from my spiritual sister in Christ, Amelda Thomas-Jones, telling me that the Lord had placed me heavy on her heart. I called my dear friend "Sister Amelda"—she was elated to hear from me finally. Apparently, she had previously called me but I didn't get the messages. Thank God for Amelda's obedience to the Holy Spirit in being steadfast in faith and discernment. She wasted no time in asking how I was doing and that the Spirit of the Lord had her interceding on my behalf for five months beginning back in April. The Holy Spirit planted God's Word according to Psalms 138:8 in her spirit, *"The Lord will perfect that which concerns…"* Von. He spoke this in a soft voice to her continuously over the five months of intercessory prayer for me. Amelda did not have any knowledge of my personal circumstances and trials that I was dealing with, including a life threatening situation with my husband that could have destroyed both of us. All Amelda knew was that the Lord had called her to pray for me based on the word He spoke to her, "The Lord is concerned for Von."

I proceeded to share the details of my trials with Amelda, and we both became humbled and speechless at the work of our All-knowing God. We gave thanks and rejoiced in God's faithfulness, mercy, and concern for His children. Glory to God in Jesus Christ for the "finished work on the Cross."

Thank You, Holy Spirit, for calling the intercessors to humble themselves in an attitude of obedience to the Spirit of the Lord with unceasing prayers. Just like the prophet Daniel encountered obstacles from the prince of Persia in receiving an answer to prayer, this same demonic obstacle tried to stop and block Amelda from praying for me. Amelda said the demonic voice would say, "Evonne has other friends to pray for her and don't bother her, she is fine." But the Spirit of the Lord arose strongly in Amelda against this lying spirit and she said, "Who is Evonne? I call her by her spiritual name, "Von." The Lord rebukes you, in Jesus' name!" The demons did not know the name Amelda called me, and therefore her spirit was quickened. Sister Amelda said, "As intercessors, we do not need to engage in a conversation with the enemy and his demonic forces; we need only to speak the Word of God. We are instructed in the Book of Jude of what to do when dealing with demonic powers, only the Lord has the authority to rebuke Satan; we don't need to talk with anything evil."

Amelda said she pressed on in confidence, praying for me in the Spirit whenever prompted by the Holy Spirit, regardless of her location or activities at the time. She heard the call to pray with faith and trusting that the Holy Spirit, Who knows the deep things of God, would carry out what was needed. In Hebrews 7:25 it states, *"…He ever lives to make intercession..."* Jesus is our High Priest and Intercessor; this is the confidence that I can have in Him. I am forever thankful for Jesus' death and resurrection. He reconciled me to my Heavenly Father and placed me in His righteousness. I will not forget His benefits and blessings. He heard my cry and answered because "He, the great I AM" was concerned about me. My character is being developed daily by God as I trust Him and live by faith in confidence that God is Who He says He is, and He will do what He says He will. The Lord answered both prayer requests: He provided and sent someone to pray for me, and He spoke His Word into my life. I am a recipient of God's precious blessings and benefits all due to the love and obedience of a prayer intercessor. I know in confidence that *"I can do all things through Christ who strengthens me."* (Philippians 4:13)

Joanna Coles
Lorton, Virginia

Trying to operate an unfamiliar power tool without instructions can prove unwise and often fatal. Likewise in ministry without proper instruction, failure is inevitable.

The Ancient Keys of Intercession has become my manual for effective ministry. After reading this book cover to cover—twice, underlining and highlighting passages, dissecting chapters and focusing on specific sections—I am fully persuaded it is the voice of the Holy Spirit through Amelda Thomas-Jones to the Body of Christ.

I apply and implement the Biblical principles from this text not only to my personal ministry, but to my local, jurisdictional, and national ministry assignments as well. This book goes beyond a nice Christian read, because it is an instrument that provides practical and fundamental, step-by-step instructions to edify the Church.

This composition shows you how to properly operate the tools in your ministry "kit" and when used properly, you will witness the glorious destiny of your church.